Jan Timman has another page-turner

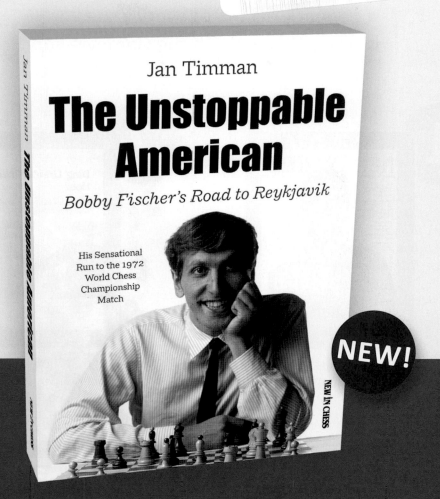

Jan Timman chronicles the full story of Bobby Fischer's dazzling run to the Match of the Century, and takes a fresh look at the games.

Fischer started out by sweeping the field at the 23-round 1970 Palma Interzonal Tournament to qualify for the next stage of the cycle. In the Candidates Matches he first trounced Soviet ace Mark Taimanov, in Vancouver. Then, a few months later in Denver, he was up against Bent Larsen. Fischer annihilated him, too. The surreal score in those two matches, twice 6-0, flabbergasted chess fans all over the world.

In the ensuing Candidates Final in Buenos Aires, Fischer also made short shrift of former World Champion Tigran Petrosian. Altogether, Fischer had scored an incredible 36 points from 43 games against many of the world's best players, including a streak of 19 consecutive wins. Bobby Fischer had become not just a national hero in the US, but a household name with pop-star status all over the world.

Another page-turner by Jan Timman, with annotations in his trademark lucid style, that happy mix of colourful background information and sharp, crystal-clear explanations.

Using the New In Chess app is easy!

- get early access to every issue
- replay all games in the Gameviewer

1

Sign in with your username and password to access the digital issue.

2

Read the article, optimized for your screen size.

3
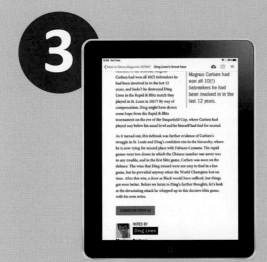
Click on the Gameviewer button to get to the built-in chess board.

4
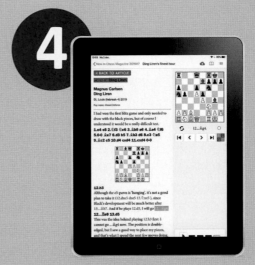
Replay the game, including an option to analyze with Stockfish.

The only chess magazine that moves
www.newinchess.com/chess-apps – for tablet, phone and PC

2021#4

NEW IN CHESS

Contents

'It is better to fail than to have never even tried'

CONTRIBUTORS TO THIS ISSUE
Simen Agdestein, Vladimir Barsky, Maxim Dlugy, Jorden van Foreest, Anish Giri, Mark Glukhovsky, Alexander Grischuk, John Henderson, Vincent Keymer, Ian Nepomniachtchi, Peter Heine Nielsen, Maxim Notkin, Judit Polgar, Matthew Sadler, Han Schut, Jan Timman, Thomas Willemze

The Chess Police

Several recent infamous incidents have led to bad community relationships with police forces across the United States. But in a new initiative from the Pittsburgh Police Community Office, they are fostering a better relationship with the public they serve simply by sitting down to play chess with them.

Each Tuesday, at noon, in Market Square in the Squirrel Hill neighborhood, Community Engagement Officers are taking on all comers, experienced and novice alike. The impromptu matches not only raise smiles but also engage with the community and break down barriers.

The initiative comes from Pittsburgh Community Resource Officer David Shifren, a lifelong chess player, after he noticed people having fun playing chess when he visited the neighborhood. On a hunch, he went to his car, pulled out his own chess set and decided to join in. So good was the local reaction and vibe to the cop playing chess that he recruited some chess-playing colleagues and armed them with new chess sets and roll-up boards. That started the weekly sessions that have become a big hit in the Downtown community.

NIC's Café

Team Nepo

You've just won the right to challenge Magnus Carlsen for his world crown, so you start to get your 'team' around you... for football-loving Ian Nepomniachtchi, that team just happened to be FC Spartak Moscow, whom he is a lifelong fan of!

Spartak were one of the first to send congratulations via a social media 'big shoutout' to their fan as Nepo won the Candidates Tournament. Not only that, but just like Magnus making his symbolic kick-off for his team, Real Madrid, Nepo similarly was invited by Spartak to do the same on his return home as the club's special VIP guest.

Maybe both Ian Nepomniachtchi and Spartak Moscow will be even happier next year.

In a warm welcome the Challenger got to meet the team, received a rousing reception from the fans and did the ceremonial kick-off. And next watched Spartak beat FC Khimki 2-1.

Space Advantage

In these challenging times of everyone and everything having to be Covid-safe, a school in China came up with a novel approach as they took all the chess action outside by utilizing the whole of a football pitch for a cup competition!

More than a thousand Shenzhen Road Primary School students based in the Liaocheng High-tech Zone took to their football field for the second 'Liangzhi Cup' in mid-April,

with the extraordinary scenes of all the competitors being perfectly socially-distanced in matching

For the Shenzhen Road Primary School students chess is also a great outdoor activity.

school tracksuits, sitting face-to-face and crosslegged in pairs.

The school has had a chess-based curriculum in place for 3 years now. 'Chess activities not only help develop children's intelligence and improve thinking skills but also cultivate good habits of tenacity, unity, and courage to challenge', commented principle Song Demin in his opening speech.

The Dark Knight

The rise of chess in popular culture through Beth Harmon now seems to have carried over to the Batman anthology. To become the ultimate crime-fighter, Bruce Wayne spent much of his formative teenage and early-adult life travelling the globe to train under the world's greatest martial arts masters. But before that journey, he first learned wisdom and

So now you know why the Dark Knight always rises.

strategy from his trusted family butler Alfred... and from playing chess, according to the latest storyline.

The April graphic novel adventure *Batman Black and White #4* includes a story called 'Checkmate', by Daniel Warren Johnson. The tale opens with Batman being easily captured by henchmen of Two-Face, with the crime boss furious that his men had walked into a trap, shouting, 'This man is only captured if he wants to be!' And sure enough, a smirk appears on the Dark Knight's face, and through a series of flashbacks we discover Alfred teaching the young Master Wayne to play chess.

As the two prepare to play, Bruce asks if he has to think multiple steps ahead in order to win, but Alfred points out that this is impossible due to the sheer amount of variables in any given game. He's also taught that 'Mastery comes from memorizing the many different situations you could be in and being prepared for each one.' As the fight rages on, the butler adds, 'And when you discover a situation you've never encountered before, you must learn to improvise.'

Then the story bounces back to the present, as Batman cunningly defeats Two-Face and his goons. On returning home to Wayne Manor, he's once again beaten at chess by his faithful butler.

Women in Power

We offer our hearty congratulations to Antoaneta Stefanova, who in April became the latest Eastern European woman grandmaster to hang up her pawns for politics after she was elected as an MP in Bulgaria's national elections!

The 2004 FIDE Women's World Champion was elected to the Bulgarian parliament as a member of the populist, anti-corruption, pro-European party Ima Takav Narod (There is Such a People), named after a song of the party founder and leader Slavi Trifonov.

2004 Women's World Champion Antoaneta Stefanova is now a member of the Bulgarian parliament.

Stefanova follows in the footsteps of her sister parliamentarians Viktorija Cmilyte-Nielsen, now the Speaker of the Seimas, the Lithuanian Parliament, and Dana Reizniece-Ozola, who formerly served as the Latvian Minister for Economics (2014-16) as well as Finance (2016-19), before announcing she would be stepping back from her parliamentary duties to take up a new role in January as Managing Director and Vice Chairperson of the Board of FIDE.

Four Queens

Four special, highly talented Georgian women were virtually neighbours, sometimes colleagues and sometimes bitter rivals, but above all, they were regarded as national heroines and pioneers of women's chess. Now the story of Nona Gaprindashvili, Nana

Chiburdanidze, Alexandria, Gaprindashvili and Ioseliani, four Georgian women that won countless medals for the Soviet Union.

Alexandria, Maia Chiburdanidze and Nana Ioseliani is set to be told in a new documentary *Glory to the Queen* (Berghammer Film, 82 minutes).

Written and directed by Tatia Skhirtladze, the Austrian/Georgian/Serbian produced film is a reminder of the four's dominance of the women's chess scene through the 1970s and 80s – before the Polgars and the rise of China's conquering women.

The film's original 2020 festival plans were upended because of the pandemic. But last September, with the four protagonists in the audience, it finally had its premier to rave reviews during the Tbilisi Film Festival.

Now *Glory to the Queen* is primed to hit the coming film festival circuit, and after that it will go on general release and soon also streaming on digital platforms – so one to definitely watch out for.

One-way Ticket

History could well be in the making for the world's youngest IM, Abhimanyu Mishra, the 12-year-old American who is frantically trying to break Sergey Karjakin's 19-year-old record set in 2002 as the youngest grandmaster at 12 years and seven months.

Abhi – as he's more affectionately known as – turned in another remarkable feat at the May edition of the First Saturday GM tournament in Budapest. Not only did he finish three points ahead of the field with an unbeaten score of 8/9, but in the process he also notched up his second successive GM norm in Hungary in as many months.

The young shooting star from New Jersey and his father, Hemant, have booked a one-way ticket to Budapest, where they'll be based over the summer in an all-out attempt to smash Karjakin's record. As his father explained to ESPN, 'He gets the third norm and we take the first

flight back home to New Jersey. Or we stay back till that happens.'

His date with destiny is set as he has to bag his final norm plus an Elo gain of around 3-4 points before 5 September. The signs are promising, as he's averaged 2550 plus for his last six tournaments.

Here's a sample from a recent game.

Levente Papp
Abhimanyu Mishra
Budapest First Saturday 2021

position after 20.♔h1

20...♖xf4! With a maturity that belies his age, young Mishra's double exchange sacrifice leaves White

Abhimanyu Mishra will not leave Budapest before he has broken Sergey Karjakin's record.

in dire straits. **21.♖xf4 ♗xf4 22.♗xf4 ♖xf4 23.gxf4 ♕xh4+ 24.♔g1 ♕xf4** With Black's queen and knights working in perfect unison, White's exposed king soon gets caught in the crossfire. **25.b3 ♘e5 26.♖a2 ♕g3** White cannot stop 27...♘g4 winning. ■

The wait is over

After 400 days Ian Nepomniachtchi wins Candidates tournament

A happy couple at the prize-giving: Ian Nepomniachtchi and his girlfriend Snezhana Fomicheva.

LENNART OOTES

More than a year had passed between the two halves of the Candidates tournament. There has never been anything like it in chess history. The tension that had built up for so many months, was essentially released in a week, as Ian Nepomniachtchi only needed five games to become Magnus Carlsen's next Challenger. **VLADIMIR BARSKY** reports from Yekaterinburg.

After the first half, which ended on 25 March 2020, first place was shared by Maxime Vachier-Lagrave and Ian Nepomniachtchi with 4½ points out of 7. The French grandmaster had won their head-to-head game, an important advantage for a possible tiebreak. Fabiano Caruana, Anish Giri, Wang Hao and Alexander Grischuk were one point behind the leaders. Finally, Ding Liren and Kirill Alekseenko were at the bottom of the table with 2½ points each.

FIDE tried several times to resume the tournament. For example, Georgia was an option last autumn, as for a long time the formidable virus had bypassed the hospitable Transcaucasian republic. But alas, in autumn Georgia left the green zone and rapidly moved into the red... At the same time, not all Candidates were eager to resume play, since the clear leaders and outsiders had already been identified, and the Russian organizers insisted that the tournament end in the same place where it had begun, that is, in Yekaterinburg.

FIDE president Arkady Dvorkovich and his team had to make huge diplomatic efforts to get everyone back together at the same time in one place. Only in April 2021, when the epidemiological situation in Russia improved, did the grandmasters, together with their seconds, arrive at the well-known Hyatt Hotel.

The strange feeling of déjà vu was best expressed, perhaps, by Anish Giri. When he saw the same hall and the same scenery, he had the feeling that not a year had passed, but only one day. With a smile, he shared his impressions of his arrival in Russia. For example, he talked about how he took off his face mask in the VIP lounge of Sheremetyevo airport to eat, then forgot to put it on, and after a while he was amazed to realize that no one was running to him and demanding that it be returned to its place. The grandmaster, whose childhood was spent in St. Petersburg, even quoted our famous 19th-century writer Mikhail Saltykov-Shchedrin: 'The severity of Russian laws is mitigated by the non-binding nature of their execution.'

Too comfortable

And yet, on the stage of the 'Hyatt' some innovations were seen. A year ago, all the grandmasters were sitting in identical green leather chairs with the logo of the general sponsor. Beautiful, solid, I would call them 'director style'. But literally the day before the tournament resumed, some participants began to complain that these chairs were not comfortable enough for them. That is, they were too comfortable, you wanted to lie down and relax in them, and not work hard for 5-6 hours. Dvorkovich listened to the complaint and allowed everyone to change their chair to their preference. And so Caruana switched to a special gaming chair, the ascetic Grischuk took an ordinary chair from the auditorium, Giri – a simple office chair, etc. Only the leaders, 'MVL' and 'Nepo', decided not 'to change horses in midstream' and retained their green seats.

A year ago, the opening ceremony was held solemnly, on a grand scale, in a huge hall. Several thousand spectators gathered and famous artists performed. You may remember the beautiful photo of Lennart Ootes of the packed hall that appeared in this magazine. In the new reality, mass events are still banned (well, not always in our country – remember the words of Saltykov-Shchedrin). The second half was opened without pathos: a few short welcoming speeches, the symbolic first moves of the guests of honour – and off you go!

A year ago, a disturbing atmosphere reigned in the Hyatt. No one really knew what kind of beast it was – this coronavirus, but everyone was terribly afraid of it. Grandmasters abandoned traditional handshakes and, at best, at the suggestion of the witty Grischuk, touched each other with their elbows. Communication with journalists was minimized, the PCR test had to be taken every day, and anyone who accidentally coughed in a public place felt like a dangerous criminal and collected frowns from all neighbours. In the city itself, on the contrary, the atmosphere was completely relaxed, you came across people wearing masks about as often as bears.

This time the atmosphere in and around the hall was much calmer and friendlier. Some had already been vaccinated, some had already been ill, some were just 'concerned'. Yes, the temperature was still measured several times a day, and the PCR test before the start had to be taken even by those who had already been vaccinated – no matter whether it was 'Sputnik', 'Pfizer' or something else. But spectators were allowed into the commentary room, where grandmasters Sergey Shipov and Mikhail Ulibin worked. The chairs were one and a half meters apart, but there were at least 40 of them, and they were practically never empty, as the audience took turns.

After finishing the games, the chess players often stayed at the tables to briefly analyse the game – just like in the good old days. And in the press centre they often joked and smiled again: it was evident that they had missed the live communication and the tournament atmosphere familiar to them.

Some participants complained that the chairs were too comfortable, you wanted to lie down and relax in them

A cautious restart

According to the rules, representatives of one country had to play their games against each other first. Therefore, two games out of four in Round 8 were between compatriots. Wang Hao and Ding Liren found a perpetual check in a sharp variation of the Scottish game in two hours. At the press conference, Wang Hao said, 'I didn't consider it necessary to practice chess for the entire past year, as I didn't have any special invitations to online tournaments. Naturally, just before the Candidates Tournament, I spent a couple of months preparing. Before that, I studied investments for quite a long time and improved my knowledge in this area.' This was a first warning, which no one then took seriously.

Alexander Grischuk, who had drawn all seven games in the first half, really wanted to break this routine in his game against Kirill Alekseenko and chose the French Defence, which during his long professional career he very rarely used in classical games. He confidently solved his opening problems, but then he overestimated his chances, several times avoided draws and in the end went too far. Kirill scored his first win and Alexander went to '-1' and practically dropped out of the struggle for first place.

But the games involving the two leaders naturally aroused particular interest. Frankly, Nepomniachtchi-Giri turned out to be boring: a draw in a Sveshnikov in less than two hours. Immediately after the game, Ian said that he had prepared for many openings, but still Anish's choice was a surprise. 'Sometimes a whole year is not enough to prepare for seven games,' Nepomniachtchi smiled. At the end of the tournament, he was more frank: he said that he did have a good idea for the Sveshnikov, but forgot to repeat it, as he had expected other openings from Giri. And he also admitted that he had trouble sleeping at the beginning of the second half.

In a clear contrast, the fight between Caruana and Vachier-Lagrave was exciting and a highpoint, not only of the 8th round, but of the entire Candidates Tournament. And it made Ian Nepomniachtchi the sole leader, half a point ahead of Caruana and MVL.

NOTES BY
Jorden van Foreest

Fabiano Caruana
Maxime Vachier-Lagrave
Yekaterinburg 2021 (8)
Sicilian Defence, Najdorf Defence

1.e4

This had been one of the most anticipated games for over a year. The entire chess world had been debating the choice of opening: If Caruana went 1.e4, would Vachier-Lagrave play his beloved Najdorf? Or would he have something else up his sleeve? After MVL's disastrous appearance in Wijk aan Zee, with many losses in the Najdorf, one of them to Caruana, he might well switch openings.

1...c5 2.♘f3 d6 3.d4 cxd4 4.♘xd4 ♘f6 5.♘c3 a6

MVL answers the question by sticking to his Najdorf! Clearly not fearing Caruana's highly dangerous opening preparation.

6.♗g5 e6 7.f4 ♕b6

The Poisoned Pawn Variation. More than half a century ago, Bobby Fischer popularized the opening, and it remains a hot topic to this day.

The line usually leads to extremely sharp variations, with a lot of theory involved. The variation is also well suited for deep computer analysis, which Caruana is known to do very well.

8.♕d2 ♕xb2 9.♖b1 ♕a3

10.e5

Caruana deviates from the game in Wijk aan Zee. There, he opted for the slightly less common 10.♗e2. This time he chooses one of the main lines. A couple of years back, in 2015, he defeated MVL with 10.f5, which is the other heavily theoretical line.

10...h6 11.♗h4 dxe5 12.fxe5 ♘fd7 13.♘e4!

Preventing the nasty pin after ...♗b4, while at the same time bringing the knight into the centre, from where it has many attacking ideas.

13...♕xa2

It may look shocking to capture another pawn on the side of the board, while seriously undeveloped, but the capture has the good point that it allows the queen to go to d5 and assist in the defence.

14.♖d1 ♕d5 15.♕e3 ♕xe5

So far this is all theory, but now

Fabiano deviates from the trodden paths.

16.c3!?

It must have been this idea that Caruana had been waiting to use. Although not a novelty, it is definitely a very rare move. MVL sunk into deep thought, clearly on his own from here on in. For now, the idea behind the text-move remains hidden. Why would this be better than the main move 16.♗e2, which seems far more useful? In a couple moves we'll find out.

16...♗c5 17.♗g3 ♛d5 18.♗c4!

A stunning bishop sacrifice, which must have come as a thunderbolt from a clear sky for MVL. Deflecting the queen from the defence of the d6-square is worth an entire piece and is the essential idea behind 16.c3.

18...♛xc4 19.♗d6!?

Black is up a piece and three pawns(!), yet he is in a precarious position. He has no development, his king is stuck in the centre and his queen can easily come under attack. Nevertheless, Black does have several ways out of the maze of complications to attain a decent position. For a while, MVL

Guest of honour Anatoly Karpov made the first move in the thriller between Fabiano Caruana and Maxime Vachier-Lagrave.

navigates the dangers very well and plays in what I believe to be the most human and practical way.

19...♘f6!

Giving back the piece in order to free his position somewhat. In the press conference, Caruana said he had hoped MVL would not find this hard move.

The greedy continuation is 19...♗xd4, when Black keeps the material advantage but loses important time. Black turns out to be objectively fine here too, but the way out of all the complications is almost impossible to find for a human player: 20.♖xd4 ♛b3 21.♛g3!.

ANALYSIS DIAGRAM

Pinpointing the pawn on g7, and as long as Black cannot castle, this is very hard to deal with. 21...♛b1+ (harassing the white king is the best way to continue; 21...♖g8 22.0-0 gives White a crushing attack, since after 22...♘c6 23.♗c7! the threat of ♘d6 is deadly) 22.♔f2 ♛c2+ (22...♛xh1? 23.♛xg7 is not recommended for Black, although it certainly does have similarities to games from old romantic times) 23.♔e3. Surprisingly, the white king finds shelter in the middle of the board, which means that Black has just one way to save the game: 23...g5! 24.♗a3 ♘c6 25.♛c7! f5!.

White has no more than move repetition here: 26.♘d6+ ♔e7 27.♘e4+ (27.♘xc8++ looks tempting, but after 27...♔f6 it would be Black who would mate!) 27...♔e8 28.♘d6+ ♔e7, with a draw.

20.♘xc5 ♘d5 21.♕e5

21...♖g8 This ugly-looking move is the point behind Black's 20th move. Black calmly defends his g7-pawn. Let's not forget that he is still up three pawns, and if he had one or two more moves, the white initiative would fade away. The time has come to strike for Caruana, but in doing so the position simplifies a lot.

22.♘dxe6!

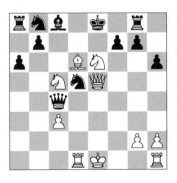

Another sacrifice to maintain the initiative.

22...fxe6 23.♘xe6 ♕xc3+ 24.♕xc3 ♘xc3 25.♘c7+ ♔f7 26.♖d3 The queens have been traded and White is down a knight and two pawns. But it's still Black who has to be accurate to preserve the balance!

26...♘e4?! MVL takes a very human approach, giving back a full rook in order to coordinate his forces and gain some time to develop his pieces at last. However, the cold-blooded 26...♖a7 would have solved all Black's problems, and the game would most likely have ended in a draw.

27.0-0+ ♔g6 28.♘xa8

28...♘c6?! Most of the smoke has cleared, and we find ourselves in a complicated endgame. White has restored material balance and seems to be slightly better. The text-move allows White to comfortably block the pawn duo on the queenside. It would have been better to bother the white pieces instead: 28...♖d8! 29.♖fd1 ♗f5 30.♗a3 ♖xd3 31.♖xd3 ♘d7 and the difference between the game is clear: White fails to block the black pawns, and although White is still slightly better, the position is rather drawish.

29.♘b6 ♖d8

Perhaps it was better to keep the bishop for some counterplay. Now the Black knights start getting dominated and despite the reduced material, the king will soon become a target.

30.♘xc8 ♖xc8

31.♗a3

Keeping the bishop and intending to reroute it to b2, from where it will be firing at the black kingside.

31...♖c7 It is essential to protect the seventh rank.

32.♖f4 ♘f6 33.♗b2 ♘e7

He has to bring back the other knight to the defence, even if it's at the cost of allowing White to ruin the pawn structure.

34.♗xf6 gxf6

35.h4?

This seems to be Caruana's only real mistake in the entire game. The move is understandable, as he is trying to attack the black king. But as we know, pawns do not move backwards, and the consequence of this move is that White permanently loses the flexibility of his pawns, and with it his control over the g4-square. MVL immediately exploits this.

35...h5!

Fixing the white pawns, and basically forcing a long forced sequence, since White cannot allow ...♘f5-h6-g4 to happen.

36.♖g3+ ♔f7 37.♖g5

Caruana finds the only way to keep the game going, using his rooks to create immediate problems for Black.

37...♖c1+ 38.♔h2 ♘g6 39.♖f2 ♘xh4 40.♖xh5 ♘g6 41.♖h7+ ♔e6 42.♖xb7

White has won a pawn, but in the process the position has become far more drawish, since two pawns have been eliminated.

42...♘e5 43.♖b6+ ♖c6!

MVL correctly judges that the ensuing endgame must be drawn.

44.♖xc6+ ♘xc6

The position is a draw, but it requires precise defending from Black. The black a-pawn is still on the board, but it will soon be lost.

45.♔g3 ♔f7 46.♖c2 ♘b4 47.♖d2 ♘c6 48.♔f4 ♔g6 49.♖d6 ♘e5?!

This is inaccurate. 49...♘e7! would have been easier, as will be explained shortly.

50.♖xa6

In the commentary room a small exhibition had been set up with highlights from Anatoly Karpov's stunning stamp collection (one of the biggest in the world).

Finally we have reached the endgame that caused such a stir. Despite looking simple, it is highly complex, the crux being in the pawn on g2. With that pawn on g4, it would be an easy draw. The fact that it is still in its starting position gives White the possibility of giving a nasty check on the g-file with ♖g3+, forcing Black to make a concession. The idea for White is then to eventually try and infiltrate with the king via either g4 or d5.

What is the defensive set-up Black should be aiming for here? It turns out that the black knight would be perfectly positioned on g7. At first, it seems surprising, but there is a logic to it, as it conveniently covers both the h5- and e6-squares, from where the white king could infiltrate into the enemy camp, only from there. This also explains why Black's 49th move was inaccurate: The knight is now at the maximum distance from square g7, complicating his defensive task.

50...♘f7 51.♔e4 ♘h6 52.♖a5 ♘f7 53.♖a3 ♘d6+ 54.♔f4 ♘f5 55.♖d3

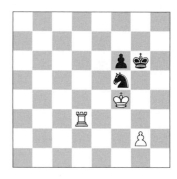

55...♘h6? 55...♘g7! would have secured the draw for the reason given above. While the knight on h6 seems to be doing a similar job covering the g4-square, it cannot hold the barrier, as we will see.

56.♖g3+!

The first step of the plan is completed. Now the king gets cut off on the g-file after either 56...♔h5 or 56...♔h7. MVL chooses 56...♔f7, which seems to block all inroads for now. But there is a way for White to break through.

56...♔f7 57.♔e4 ♘g8 58.♔f5

It seems as though Caruana had not yet seen the winning plan, and in fact he will give Black one more chance to escape.

58...♘e7+ 59.♔f4 ♘d5+ 60.♔g4 ♔g6 61.♔f3+ ♔f7 62.♔e4

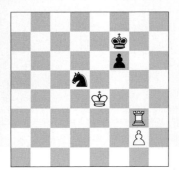

62...♘e7?

This really is the final mistake, after which Caruana spots the winning plan and is ruthless in its execution. The only way to draw was once again to bring the knight back to g7, starting with 62...♘c7!, intending either ...♘e8 or ...♘e6.

63.♔f4 ♘d5+ 64.♔f5!

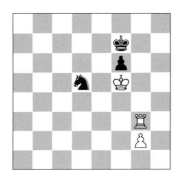

The only winning move, stopping ...♘c7 !

64...♘e7+

64...♘c7 65.♖d3 doesn't work now for Black, as a nasty check from d7 is in the air.

65.♔e4 ♘g8 66.♖h3 ♔g6 67.♖a3 ♔f7 68.♔f4 ♘h6 69.♖g3!

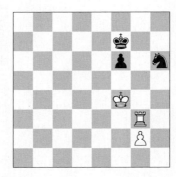

The position that Caruana was aiming for. Amazingly, Black is in zugzwang and cannot hold the barrier. In fact, if we compare the position with the one after Black's 56th move, we see that it is the same, with one key difference: It is now Black to move instead of White! This is why this defensive set-up fails. As for Black's moves, ...f5 is obviously equivalent to capitulation. Any of the king moves allows ♖g6, so there is only the knight left. However, as we know now, moving the knight allows the white king to enter the enemy camp.

69...♘g8 70.♔g4! ♘e7 71.♔h5

The king enters decisively.

71...♘d5 72.♖f3 ♔e6 73.g4 ♔e5 74.♔g6

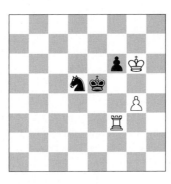

MVL threw in the towel, as he will soon lose the f6-pawn.

74...♔e6 75.♖f1 ♘e7+ 76.♔g7 ♘d5 77.♖e1+ ♔d6 78.♖d1 would be a sample line in which Black's defences collapse. The unstoppable threat of ♖xd5, followed by ♔xf6, will give White a winning king and pawn endgame.

An amazingly complicated struggle and a great fight.

∎ ∎ ∎

Russian Roulette

After his unfortunate defeat on the first day, Grischuk really wanted to defeat Nepomniachtchi in Round 9 and even at some point 'played roulette', choosing an objectively dubious continuation. Ian understood that his opponent was bluffing, but failed to find a clear path to an advantage (at the press conference, he said, sincerely or not very much so, that after accepting the exchange sacrifice he did not even see clear equality). Following a long think Nepomniachtchi opted for caution and the game ended in a draw.

MVL again did not live up to his role of one of the favourites and was on the verge of a second defeat against Ding Liren. The Frenchman's escape was a small miracle.

Fabiano Caruana had chances to win a second victory, but Kirill Alekseenko, finding himself in an unpleasant situation, successfully muddied the waters and this game also ended in a draw.

Meanwhile, Anish Giri scored a technical victory over Wang Hao and entered the race for the lead.

NOTES BY
Anish Giri

Anish Giri
Wang Hao
Yekaterinburg 2021 (9)
Catalan Opening, Closed Variation

1.d4 ♘f6 2.c4 e6 3.♘f3 d5 4.g3 ♗e7

Wang Hao is very solid against all

openings, and the Catalan isn't an exception. This is the classical system, in which Black chooses to stay somewhat passive, but it is incredibly solid and robust; the favourite of Vladimir Kramnik.

5.♗g2 0-0 6.0-0 dxc4 7.♕c2 a6

8.a4 In the past, the theoretical debate mainly revolved around the position after 8.♕xc4 b5 9.♕c2 ♗b7 10.♗d2!, but by now Black has solved his opening problems there. With a4 White stops the ...b7-b5 push, but weakens the b4-square and loses some time.

8...♗d7 The problem for Black in this line is his c8-bishop, and now that ...b5 has been prevented, solving the development problem this way is the most common option.

9.♕xc4 ♗c6

10.♗f4

The idea is that the natural 10.♘c3 is met by ...b5-b4!, so White usually develops the bishop first. Alternatively, 10.♗g5 is also a major move that I have tried a bunch of times.

10...♗d6

Old theory used to be 10...a5, followed by ...♘a6, but the move Hao played is

Anish Giri entered the race for the lead with a fine technical win over Wang Hao.

the trendiest. Black hints at trading the bishops.

11.♘c3

Previously, I followed the main paths and used to address the issue of ...♗xf4 either with 11.♗g5 or with the cunning 11.♕c1!?. Both of these options remain critical, but for this game I wanted to try this somewhat rare move, hoping to catch Hao off guard. And indeed, he started taking some time.

11...♗xf4 Principled. **12.gxf4 a5**

In this system, Black often chooses between ...a5, followed by ...♘a6, and ...♘bd7. Both have their pros and cons, but sticking the knight

on the weak b4-square is definitely tempting.

13.e3 ♘a6 14.♘e5 Offering another trade of bishops. So far, this has all been played before, though the highest-rated encounter So-Navara saw Wesley not trade the bishops yet but go for ♔h1 and ♖g1 first.

14...♗xg2 15.♔xg2 c6

Hao keeps the knight on a6 (instead of 15...♘b4) and retains the option of challenging the centre with ...c5. I had studied this position enough to know that the ...c5 break often fails to solve all the problems, as the weakness of the b5-square will be felt and the e5-knight becomes only more

Tani Adewumi: 'When you lose, you have made a mistake, and that can help you learn. I never lose. I learn.' *(The 10-year-old former Nigerian refugee, interviewed by The New York Times in April, after he became one of the youngest US National Masters)*

Alexander Grischuk: 'Did you watch the film *In Bruges*? There's a quote there that applies to me: "They weren't really shit, but they weren't all that great either, like Tottenham!"' *(In an interview with the Russian media on the eve of leaving for the resumed Candidates in Yekaterinburg)*

A.A. Milne: 'Chess has this in common with making poetry; that the desire for it comes upon the amateur in gusts.' *(The chess-loving author of Winnie The Pooh)*

Magnus Carlsen: 'In other news, the ocean is full of water!' *(During the Candidates, when quizzed about Alexander Grischuk being down to 3 minutes to make 16 moves)*

Hikari Yokoyama: 'The best gift I've given recently is a vintage Bakelite Soviet-Arabic chess clock, which I bought for Jay from Design Fornication in Vienna. Playing to a timer, rather than freely, changes the whole chess game. I started playing at school in the third grade, then went dormant as it was seen as nerdy. Now it's a favourite pastime of ours.' *(The celebrated American art curator, in The Financial Times about the gift she recently gave to her equally chess-addicted art mogul husband, Jay Jopling)*

Zaven Collins: 'I envision myself as a chess piece they can use in many ways.' *(The new Arizona Cardinals recruit's thoughts on his strategic selection in the NFL draft)*

Rainn Wilson: 'I would probably beat Magnus if it had an optional "foetal Magnus Carlsen."' *(The US comedian and chess addict making a surprise guest appearance during the New In Chess Classic, using the Play Magnus App, and lasting only 30 moves against 10-year-old Magnus Carlsen)*

Michio Kaku: 'The universe in some sense is like a chess game, and for 2,000 years we've been trying to figure out how the pawns move. And now we're beginning to understand how the queen moves and how you get a checkmate. The destiny of science is to become like grandmasters, to solve this puzzle that we call the universe.' *(The professor of physics, string theorist and bestselling author in an interview with The Guardian)*

Juan José Arreola: 'When I lose [at chess] I feel that the world is no longer stable. These rooms that seem solid lose their solidity and wobble, or at least lose their horizontal axes and go out of frame. There is a bewilderment, and that bewilderment originates from the fact that our internal core has been shaken, it has been altered.' *(The Mexican writer and humorist, interviewed in the October 1997 edition of Ajedrez de Mexico on his passion for the game)*

Marcel Duchamp: 'Chess is a school of silence... When we talk it's usually nonsense.'

Boris Gelfand: 'It's important to understand what's the lesson, because it's easy to say I was unlucky, and I'm sure many players do it, and then they're unlucky their whole career!' *(The former title challenger on the painful lessons learned of his Candidates matches vs. Nigel Short & Anatoly Karpov in the early 90s)*

Michael Basman: 'If we are to elevate the game of chess to a popular sport, grandmasters must become gladiators, otherwise the game will languish on the periphery, a voice crying in the wilderness, condemned to live and die on a cold arctic shore.' *(The veteran and outspoken English IM, who recently turned 75)*

Vladimir Kramnik: 'To me somehow I felt like it's a reincarnation of Vishy, even if Vishy is still there and still playing chess!' *(On 15-year-old Indian prodigy Praggnanandhaa, the winner of the Polgar Challenge)*

Max Euwe: 'Alekhine is a poet who creates a work of art out of something that would hardly inspire another man to send home a picture postcard.'

powerful once the d-file gets opened.

16.h3 White usually goes for the ♔h1/♖g1 plan here. This subtle move allows the option of ♔h2 instead, which is ever so slightly different.

16...♕b6

Clearly hinting at ...c5. Fine by me.

17.♕e2 Really not resisting the ...c5 plan, which I felt was mistimed.

17...c5

18.♖fd1 This decision, and a few subsequent ones, took me a long time. I assumed that I was better, even if nothing special had happened and we just traded the c-pawn for the d-pawn and my pieces enjoyed all the standard squares. The forcing ♕b5!?, now and two moves later, was incredibly tempting:

18.♕b5 ♕xb5 19.axb5 (taking with the knight leads to a slightly better endgame, but then I'd probably rather keep the queens on) 19...cxd4 20.bxa6 dxc3 21.axb7 ♖ab8 22.bxc3 ♖xb7 23.♖xa5.

ANALYSIS DIAGRAM

At first I thought this was good enough, but as I started digging a bit deeper, I realized that Black will easily hold: 23...♘e4! 24.c4 and now

both 24...♖c8, followed by ...f6, and 24...♖b2!? seemed good enough to hold. Being in a must-win situation, I couldn't afford to give my opponent such an easy life.

18...cxd4

Logical, as the natural 18...♖fd8 would now be met by 19.♕b5!, when the queen swap loses for Black. However, the computer points out that it was not the end of the world, and 18...♖fd8! 19.♕b5 ♕c7! was a better attempt to keep White's advantage as small as possible.

19.♖xd4 ♖ad8

20.♖xd8!?

Another very hard decision. 20.♖ad1 is the simplest option, but then, after 20...♖xd4 21.♖xd4 ♘c7!, I wasn't sure whether it yielded anything.

Here 20.♕b5 seemed even more tempting, but again I decided to avoid simplifying, even though I believed it would give me a better endgame.

I spent loads of time on 20.♕b5!? ♕xb5 21.axb5 ♖xd4 22.exd4 ♘c7! (the right square) 23.♖xa5.

ANALYSIS DIAGRAM

And here I considered two options:

– 23...♖a8!. Black exploits the fact

that White's pawn structure is shattered and goes for an acceptable knight ending. 24.♖xa8+ ♘xa8 25.♘c4. I honestly didn't see how exactly Black was going to hold this, as b6 looked like a threat, and 25...b6? would be met by 26.f5! exf5 27.d5!, but my intuition didn't betray me. Black does hold: 25...♘f8!, and apparently 26.b6 is not such a big deal. The pawn is very weak there and the fact that the knight is temporarily locked in the corner is more of an aesthetic issue than a real one.

– 23...b6 24.♖a7 ♘fd5 25.♘xd5 ♘xd5 at first seemed solid for Black, but then I realized that White has huge winning chances. I calculated the simple 26.♖b7, but the fancy 26.f5! looks even stronger.

20...♕xd8! Hao stays afloat. The natural 20...♖xd8 allows 21.♕b5, and the a5-pawn may suddenly fall.

After 20...♖xd8 21.♕b5 ♕c7 22.♘c4! there is actually no way to save the a5-pawn.

21.♖d1 ♕a8!?

Odd, but really not bad. The queen is okay there, and does a fine job defending the queenside pawn weaknesses. Also, right now there is an X-ray to the king on g2.

22.♔g1

I was very proud of this move, as compared to the natural 22.♔h2, the f2-pawn is protected, which may come in handy once things get concrete and the black knight appears on e4 or the black queen on d2.

22.♕b5 ♘c7! was a bummer, as the white queen has no attractive square to go to.

22...♘b4

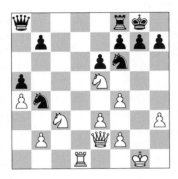

Somewhere around here I started wondering where my advantage was and whether I had any left at all. I kind of regretted not having gone for ♕b5 on move 20.

23.♕b5 I had high hopes for my queen here, but as Black is firmly guarding the a5- and b7-pawns, I didn't exactly see how to add more pressure and gain something tangible.
23...♘bd5 24.♘xd5 ♘xd5

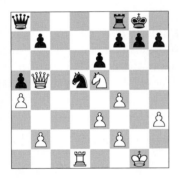

25.♖c1
The – kind of – original intention was 25.♘c4, but by now I had long realized that 25...b6! would solve Black's problems. Without much enthusiasm I decided to just continue playing.
25...h6
A fine move. In hindsight, though, maybe 25...♖d8 would have been a good option as well, stopping ♕d7 altogether. I was hoping for 25...b6, when I could offer a queen trade with 26.♕c6 at some point and aim for a better endgame, but there is no reason for Black to do this voluntarily, without White attacking the a5-pawn.

26.♕d7!? I didn't see whether I had anything more than move repetition, but there were some tricks, so I decided to try and send my queen in.
26...♘f6 26...♘b6 was not an easy solution either: 27.♕d6 ♕d8! 28.♘xf7!?. This looks like a winning tactic, but the line continues:

As Wang Hao started to think more and more, I realized that he was under quite some pressure again

28...♔xf7 29.♖c7+ ♔g8 30.♕xb6 ♖f7! (provoking ♖xb7 first) 31.♖xb7 ♕d1+ 32.♔h2 ♕f3, and White can't avoid a perpetual.
27.♕d6! Obviously not repeating with 27.♕e7 ♘d5. Here I thought Black was still completely fine, but as Hao started to think more and more, I realized that he was under quite some pressure again.

27...g6?? One question mark for the strength of the move and another for

the time my opponent spent making it. Black weakens the kingside tremendously and left himself with just seconds on the clock.
27...♘d5 was the move I had expected at first, having missed a strong resource for myself: 28.f5! ♖d8 29.♘d7!. The knight does a great job here, blocking the rook, and Black has nothing better than to go for a passive defence with 29...♖e8.
27...♕e8! was the way to go: 28.b3 b5 29.♕c6. I would have gone for the endgame by now, but it is really not much: 29...bxa4 30.♕xe8 ♖xe8 31.bxa4 ♘d5, and Black is solid, intending ...♖a8-a7 next, guarding the a5-pawn if needed.
28.b3!

I actually didn't see a good move for either of us and decided to just make a waiting one, not realizing how huge my advantage had suddenly become.
28...h5 Black is running out of moves. **29.♔h2!** Another good one. As ...♘e4xf2 is impossible, this is an excellent waiting move, not to mention some ♖g1 ideas. **29...♔g7**

The game has clearly turned heavily in my favour. Not only does White have a bunch of attractive options, Hao was also playing on increments here and was barely in time to complete his moves. Still, he was completing them and, to win the game, I had to pose him some real problems.

30.♕d4 Setting up a nasty pin. 30.♕b6! would have been a forced win, although I have to say I didn't really consider gifting Black the move ...♘d5 for free: 30...♘d5 31.♕d4!.

ANALYSIS DIAGRAM

It turns out that Black is facing concrete issues. 31...f6 is met by 32.♘d7!, and if 32...♖d8 then 33.♘xf6! wins, followed by 34.♖c7+, while if 31...♔h7, then 32.e4! cracks the position, kicking the knight away from d5 and playing ♖c7 next.

30...♖d8 31.♕b2 ♕b8

My original intention here was some ♘f3-g5 rerouting, trying to use the pin, but then I spotted the idea of 32.b4, followed by a very elegant rook lift, and didn't hesitate for a second. Objectively, though, it was a big mistake, as it allows a miraculous escape. Fortunately, he failed to find it in his few remaining seconds.

32.b4? 32.♕c3! was the winning move. I didn't really consider going after the pawn this way, because I thought the queen was one piece I shouldn't be improving, as it already does a great job paralyzing the f6-knight. But after 32...♘d5 33.♕xa5 Black has no compensation for the pawn at all and 33...f6 34.♘f3 g5 wouldn't work after 35.♕c5!, after which ...gxf4 can always be met by e4.

32...axb4 33.♖c4

33...b3? Typical, actually. Dropping to the very final seconds and not seeing a defence, Black decided to postpone a decision for one more move.

He should have gone 33...♖d1!. Obviously, I saw Black trying to set up some counterattack, but I was convinced it wouldn't work. But I was wrong, as Black has a beautiful draw here down the main line: 34.♖xb4 (this was obviously the plan) 34...♕d8 35.♖xb7 ♕d5 (setting up a couple of checks) 36.♖xf7+ ♔h6 37.♖xf6.

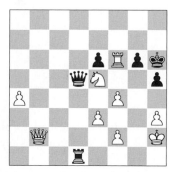

ANALYSIS DIAGRAM

I don't know if Hao had seen this far, but even if he had, he would have had to look further: 37...♖h1+! 38.♔g3 ♖xh3+!! 39.♔xh3 ♕h1+ 40.♔g3 h4+! 41.♔g4 ♕g2+, and it's a perpetual. Not too hard, as all the moves were checks, but you do have

RETURNING TO IN-PERSON TOURNAMENTS WASN'T EASY

to see it all the way in advance and we both obviously missed it.

34.罝b4

Still, a defence had to be calculated.

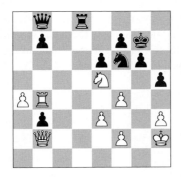

34...豐a7?

This is just losing. He had to play 34...豐d6! when White has to reply 35.豐xb3! (after 35.罝xb7 there is 35...豐d2!, and the fact that the rook can't return in time: 36.罝xf7+ 含g8 37.豐xd2 罝xd2 38.罝xf6 罝xf2+! – forcing the king to the g-file and blocking the 罝xg6-罝g1 return – 39.含g3 b2, and Black queens and holds) 35...豐d2 36.含g2!, and White keeps a large advantage, but the game goes on.

35.罝xb3 豐xa4 36.罝xb7 豐e8

37.罝a7!

It's an interesting question whether the position after 37.罝xf7+ is a fortress, and, since most likely it's not, how easy it is to win it. Not a relevant question, though, as White has a few more straightforward wins. 37.e4 looked great as well.

37...罝d5 I was mainly hoping for 37...罝b8 38.豐c2!, winning on the spot, due to two threats: 罝xf7+ and 豐xg6!+. This move loses as well.

38.豐b7

Black can't even give up an exchange here, as after 38...罝xe5 39.fxe5 he will lose more material with 罝a8 coming.

38...公e4 39.公xf7

Black resigned. An important victory.

■ ■ ■

Standings after Round 9:
1. Nepomniachtchi 5½ points, 2-4. Giri, Vachier-Lagrave, Caruana 5.

A happy 'Semi-Catalan'

In the two previous rounds, Ian Nepomniachtchi had looked somewhat constrained. I have known him for 20 years, and he has always been famous for his ease of decision making. And I am not talking about children's competitions, where Ian often spent half an hour on an entire game. In December last year, he won the Russian Championship, acting in his usual manner, every now and then pushing his opponent into time trouble. But now, in Yekaterinburg, he suddenly began to play very solidly. With great caution. And, most importantly, slowly.

What is this burden of responsibility? Does the proximity of a lofty goal fetter your creative impulses? Round 10 was supposed to clarify the situation. Having the white pieces against not the most dangerous opponent in the field: when else to go forward, if not now? To be honest, I was hoping to see another opening 'bomb', as in December against Karjakin. However, potent means were not needed: Ian was helped by psychology and the effect of foresight.

Ian Nepomniachtchi
Kirill Alekseenko
Yekaterinburg 2021 (10)
Semi-Catalan

1.c4

Like any top player, Ian has a very wide opening repertoire, but he still uses this move much less often than 1.e4 or 1.d4.

1...公f6 2.g3 e6 3.奧g2 d5 4.公f3 dxc4 5.豐a4+ 公bd7 6.豐xc4 a6 7.豐c2 c5 8.公c3

The so-called 'Semi-Catalan' (the white pawn lingers on d2 and so far postpones its decision of where to go – to d4 or d3) is a rather tricky scheme. Outwardly, everything looks dignified and noble: White sets his sights on a long, viscous positional struggle 'full of nuances'. But as soon as Black hesitates a little, the game opens up and White, due to the advantage in development, creates serious pressure.

8...奧e7?!

As Kirill admitted, he didn't remember the line that had arisen very well, he hadn't repeated it before the game. The unhurried development of the king's bishop is a serious inaccuracy. Instead, as in the 'real' Catalan, it was necessary to urgently take care of the c8-bishop. The immediate 8...b5 does not work because of 9.公e5, but here is a fresh recipe from

Potent means were not needed: Ian was helped by psychology and the effect of foresight

Andrey Esipenko: 8...♕c7 9.0-0 b6 10.d4 ♗b7 11.♗f4 ♗d6 12.♗xd6 ♕xd6 13.♖fd1 0-0 with comfortable play for Black, Donchenko-Esipenko, Wijk aan Zee 2021.

9.0-0 0-0 10.d4 cxd4?

It seems that Black's position holds after 10...b5!?, but it is hardly possible to decide on this without preparation: it is necessary to reckon with 11.♘e5, and 11.♘g5, and 11.dxc5 – everywhere White has a strong initiative...

11.♘xd4

One involuntarily recalls the famous game Kasparov-Petrosian, Bugojno 1982, of which young Garry was very proud. Now White has a big positional advantage 'for free'. Alekseenko, of course, is a very inventive chess player, but here he was powerless too.

11...♕c7 12.♖d1 ♖d8 13.♗e3 ♘b6 14.♖ac1 e5

It is easy and simple to play for White: be aware of placing your pieces in the centre, in striking positions. Black, on the other hand, has to make serious concessions to complete his development.

15.♘f5

Ian Nepomniachtchi has reached a dream position and Kirill Alekseenko knows it.

15...♗xf5

At the press conference Ian was asked how he was going to continue in case of 15...♗f8. The point is that the computer happily lights up the spectacular blow 16.♘xg7!, promising White a big advantage in all variations. Here is one of them: 16...♔xg7 (16...♗xg7 17.♘e4) 17.♕b3! ♘c4 18.♖xd8 ♘xe3 19.♖xf8 ♔xf8 20.fxe3. According to Nepomniachtchi, he saw this resource and, most likely,

would have studied it more closely, although in general he did not think that the position required such 'surgical' decisions. Indeed, White has a wide choice here, for example, 16.♗g5 or 16.♖xd8 ♕xd8 and now 17.♗g5.

After the exchange of the light-squared bishop, Black has a strategically difficult position; he can only hope for some tricks.

16.♕xf5 ♘c4 17.♗g5 ♖xd1+ 18.♘xd1 ♖d8 19.♗xf6 ♗xf6 20.♗e4 ♕a5

21.♘c3!

The h7-pawn will not run anywhere. Ian finds the most technical way to

the goal, depriving Black of even the slightest counterplay.

21...♗f8 22.♘d5 b5

If 22...♖xd5 23.♗xd5 ♕xd5, then 24.♕c8+ ♔e7 25.♖xc4.

23.♕xh7

When the computer colours a move deep red, as in this case, the viewer flinches: has the grandmaster really missed something? But no, Ian calculated everything clearly. He also saw the move 23.♖c3 (the strongest, according to the electronic mind), but considered it unnatural, too 'computerized'.

23...♖xd5 24.♗xd5 ♕d2 25.♖xc4 bxc4

26.e4! White not only strengthens his centralized bishop, but also deprives his opponent of the opportunity to 'drop' the e5-pawn in order to revive his own bishop.

26...♕xb2 27.♕h8+ ♚e7 28.♕c8

28...♕b6 He has to take the queen to the defence, because after 28...♕xa2 29.♕c7+ ♚e8 30.♗c6+ everything ends with checkmate.

29.♕xc4 ♕b5 30.♕c7+ ♕d7 31.♕c5+ Black resigns: he also loses the f7-pawn, after which he will have no chance of salvation.

Ian Nepomniachtchi: 'From a purely optical point of view, it may seem that it was a very easy game for me, but in reality, of course, it was not so. I think I was lucky that in the opening Kirill quickly got into an unfamiliar position.'

The other three games ended in a draw, and Ian Nepomniachtchi increased his lead to a full point.

Without burning bridges

One full point ahead four rounds before the finish is a serious claim for success. Ian Nepomniachtchi, playing with White against one of his closest pursuers, Fabiano Caruana, did not take any risks and after 1.e4 e5 chose the 'reinforced concrete' variation, located at the opening junction between the Four Knights and the Scotch Game. The vice-World Champion tried to complicate the struggle with a pawn sacrifice, but White had few opportunities to make a mistake. At some point, Fabiano rushed to exchange queens, after which he himself ran into problems. However, he overcame them with a careful defence, and immediately after the time control the players agreed to a draw.

'There are still three rounds left, and I thought: why burn bridges?' answered Caruana when asked why he played 1...e5, and did not choose something sharper.

And Ian said: 'You can call my opening choice tournament strategy, but I expected Fabiano to play the Sicilian Defence or some other sharp line. 1.e4 e5 is a very solid continuation, where in general, if the opponent is well prepared, equal positions are obtained everywhere. I don't think

Ian Nepomniachtchi did not take any risks and after 1.e4 e5 chose the 'reinforced concrete' variation

Black had any problems in this game, except perhaps the endgame, which turned out to be quite tricky, but also nothing special.'

The other three games also began with the king's pawn move – this was the most popular way to start the game in Yekaterinburg. Grischuk scored his first victory in the Candidates Tournament, and MVL practically dropped out of the race for first place with a second loss. The winner of the best game of the event provided the comments.

NOTES BY
Alexander Grischuk

Alexander Grischuk
Maxime Vachier-Lagrave
Yekaterinburg 2021 (11)
Sicilian Defence, Closed Variation

As I arrived for the second half of the Candidates tournament, I thought I needed to beat both Ian Nepomniachtchi and Maxime Vachier-Lagrave as White in order to have a realistic chance of winning the whole thing. Alas, I had already made a draw with Nepomniachtchi, but I still had to try to beat Maxime, of course.

1.e4 c5 2.♘c3 d6 3.d4 cxd4 4.♕xd4 ♘c6 5.♕d2 g6 6.b3 ♗h6 7.f4 ♘f6 8.♗b2 e5

9.♘ge2 Typical modern preparation. White makes some useless move [instead of 9.g3 – ed.]), allowing Black to solve his problems in multiple ways. But no matter how manifold those ways are, their amount is still limited, and armed with phenomenal memory (and extensive preparation, of course) White tries to make Black play against a computer for a few more moves.

9...0-0 10.0-0-0 ♗e6 A very fine move, made quickly by Maxime. Had he also analysed 9.♘ge2 ?!

11.♚b1 a5! 12.a4 Kind of a critical position. 'Kind of', because most reasonable moves are actually fine for Black. However, he cannot solve his problems by one or two precise moves; he has to continue to play accurately in most lines.

12...♕b6 A fine move, too, but slightly on the dangerous side.

13.h4! ♖ac8 14.h5 ♘xh5 15.g3
During the game, I was pretty sure that Maxime had done something wrong already. This is not the case at all, but five moves later I was completely winning. Optimism helps!

15...♘b4 16.♗h3

16...♗xh3
Speaking of phenomenal memory, I had 16...♖c6, with subsequent equality, in my notes, but didn't have the slightest clue about it during the game!

17.♖xh3 ♗g7?
The first real mistake. 17...♕f2! 18.♖dh1 exf4 would still be OK for Black.

18.g4! Now White takes over.

18...♘f6
18...♘xf4 19.♘xf4 exf4 20.♕xf4 (but not 20.♖dh1, as I had planned, in view of 20...♕d4! 21.♖xf4 ♘d5!) is also sad for Black.

19.g5

19...♘h5?
Now Black is dead lost. Good or bad (bad!), he had to play 19...♘g4, when I had planned 20.♖f1, which is the best move indeed. However, after 20...♘f2! 21.♖f3 ♘g4!

ANALYSIS DIAGRAM

Black is still kicking. Here White would have to find 22.♖g1! f5! 23.♘d5! ♗xd5 24.♕xd5+ ♔h8 25.exf5 ♘e3! 26.♖xe3! ♕xe3 27.f6 ♕xe2 28.fxg7+ ♔xg7 29.♖c1 ♖f7 30.♕xd6 to claim that he is winning, and even then the fight still goes on after 30...♔g8.

20.f5
At this point I took a long think, managing to calculate 10+ moves deep. However, I missed an extremely important detail, and hadn't left myself enough time to deal with it. Time management...

20...♖fd8 21.f6 ♗f8

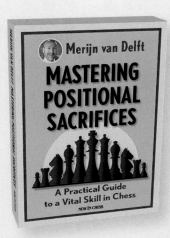

22.♘g3

The cleanest and most aesthetically pleasant win was 22.♕e1, transferring the queen to h1. From there it will attack along the h-file (White will threaten ♖xh5 gxh5, ♕xh5) and support the d5-pawn after an eventual ...d5 exd5. Actually, I was trying to find a way to bring my queen to the h-file, but the e1-h1 route didn't come to my mind. However, the text-move is fine as well.

22...d5 23.exd5 ♘xg3

Obviously, 23...♘f4 would run into 24.♖xh7!.

24.♖xg3 h5

25.♕e2

I certainly don't understand some things in chess. I thought that 25.gxh6 ♕xf6 (26.♖gg1, 26.♕g2, 26.♕h2, etc., etc.) was quite unclear, whereas the computer indicates that White is *completely* (+5 and

counting) winning after any reasonable move here.

One thing that consoles me is that Maxime actually shared my assessment, and not the computer's. Also, as I said earlier, 'I had a plan, and I was following it.'

25...♖c5 Black could try to stop White's plan of ♖h1, ♖gh3, ♖xh5 by playing 25...♕a6, but after 26.♕e4 White has complete control in the centre, and Black's king is still under the guillotine.

26.♖h3

Now 26.♖h1 ♕a6! is not so clear.

26...♘xd5 27.♘xd5 ♖cxd5 28.♖dh1 ♕d6 29.♔a2

29...♖d1!

This is the detail I had missed, as I was mostly savouring the consequences of 29...♖d2 30.♖xh5, and White checkmates.

30.♖xh5 gxh5

One thing that consoles me is that Maxime actually shared my assessment, and not the computer's

31.♖xh5?? I didn't have much time left. I saw that 31.♖h3 was tempting, but the text-move looked completely winning to me. Indeed, after 31.♖h3! ♖a1+ (strictly the only move. The major difference is that after 31...♖d4 32.♗xd4 ♕a3+ 33.♔b1 ♖xd4 34.♕xh5 the white queen controls the d1-square) 32.♗xa1 ♕d1 33.♕xd1 ♖xd1 34.♗xe5

ANALYSIS DIAGRAM

White has an easily won endgame. An important detail is 34...♔h7 35.♖xh5+ ♔g6 36.♖h8!, attacking the bishop.

31...♖d4!!

A bolt from the blue! At first I could not even understand what the rook was doing there.

'Armed with phenomenal memory (and extensive preparation, of course)', Alexander Grischuk managed to defeat Maxime Vachier-Lagrave in a wonderfully exciting game.

LENNART OOTES

37...Rd2 37...Rxe5?? 38.Qg2+ Kh7 39.Qh2+ was the trick.
38.Bc3 Re2
Now we have a forced sequence.
39.Qc8 Rg1+ 40.Kb2 Rgg2 41.Bxa5 Rxc2+ 42.Qxc2

42...Rxc2+
The last critical moment. The key in the forthcoming endgame is the b7-square. If the black king gets there, it's a draw, and if it doesn't, White wins. So, of course, it made sense to play 42...Ba3+ 43.Kb1 Rxc2 44.Kxc2 Kf8.

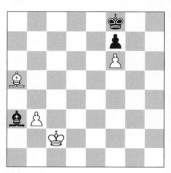

ANALYSIS DIAGRAM

At the press conference, my opponent said that he had seen it but thought there was no difference. The route g8-f8-e8-d7-b7-c7 (five moves) vs g8-h7-g6-f5-e6-d7-c7-b7 (seven moves), hmm... I know Maxime studied math in university. I sure hope it was not geometry! Seriously, though, White wins even here, but he needs to make six only moves: 45.Kc3! Ke8 46.Bb4! Bc1 47.Kc4! Kd7 48.Kb5! Bb2 49.Be7! Kc7 50.Ka6!, and the b-pawn is ready to advance.
43.Kxc2 Kh7 44.Kd3

32.Rh1 Played with around seven seconds on the clock.
The point of 31...Rd4!! is 32.Qh2 Rxa4+ 33.bxa4 Qe6+ 34.Kb1 Rd1+ 35.Bc1 Qb6+ 36.Ka2 Qe6+ 37.Kb1, with a perpetual.
32...Rxa4+ 33.Kb1

33...Qd5 Of course, Maxime had seen the line 33...Rh4 34.Rxh4 Qd1+ 35.Qxd1 Rxd1+ 36.Ka2, with complete equality, but he managed to convince himself that he would have some chances of winning with two rooks for the queen. Optimism does not always help!
34.Qh5 Qxh1+ 35.Qxh1 Rg4 36.Bxe5

36...Rxg5? 36...b5, or 36...a4, or 36...Re8 would still be a draw.
37.Qxb7!

I am also capable of cheap tricks! Maxime missed this when he decided to go for this position.

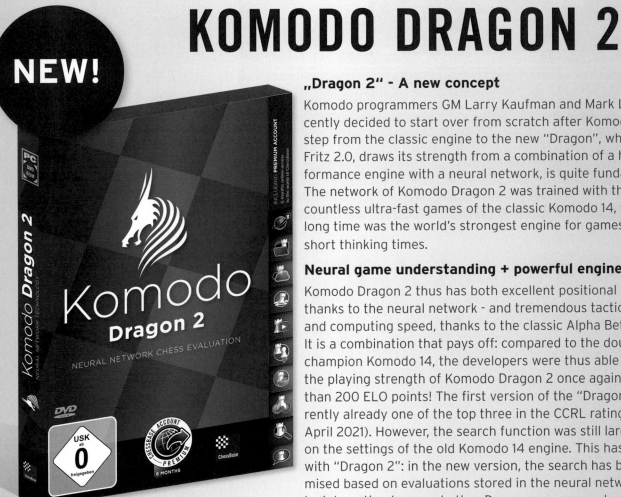

Ding Liren played brilliantly against Anish Giri in the opening phase, but lost the initiative when he rushed his attack.

the enemy king as soon as possible. The pawn does not really matter; moreover, in the event of an exchange on b4, the a-file is opened, and Black will have to reckon with the sacrifice of the rook on a6 (after d3-d4).

18.♗xc5 ♕f7 19.♖ab1 g5 20.exf5

20...g4? Ding has played the first half of the game very powerfully (Anish admitted that Black's non-standard idea with ...c7-c6 and the transfer of the bishop to c7 had been unexpected for him), and then ruined everything with one careless move. He spent only a couple of minutes here, although he had no trace of time trouble.

He had to go 20...♕xf5 in order to play 21...g4 in response to 21.♘bd2 with all the comfort. Of course, White is obliged to prevent this break by playing 21.♕e4, but the queen is a bad blocker, and after 21...♕f6! with the idea of ...♗g6, ...h5 and ...g4, Black retains a dangerous initiative.

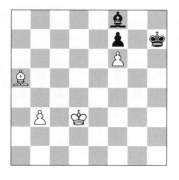

Now it is easy.

44...♔g6 45.♗c3 ♔f5 46.♔c4 ♔e6 47.b4 ♗d6

In the meantime, Anish Giri, who effectively mated Ding Liren, reduced the gap with the leader to half a point. Nevertheless immediately after the game Anish himself was not too happy with his play: 'Several people have already told me that it was a great game, but I don't think it was as good as it looked in the end. At some point, my opponent controlled the situation on the board and dictated the course of the game.'

Anish Giri
Ding Liren
Yekaterinburg 2021 (11)

position after 17.♗e3

17...f5!?
In a sharp position with opposite castling, it is important to attack

48.b5! 48.♔b5 ♔d5 was actually tricky. White would only win thanks to 49.♔b6! ♔c4 50.♔c6!.
Now Black resigned in view of 48...♔d7 49.♔d5.

∎ ∎ ∎

21.♘g5!
Ding Liren admitted that he had missed the ♘g5 and h4 manoeuvres. If White exchanged on g4 or after 21.♘h2 gxh3 22.g4 ♖hg8 Black would have excellent attacking chances.

21...♕xf5 22.h4 b6?!
Another pseudo-active move, after which Black's position collapses before our eyes. Good advice is already expensive here, but nevertheless it made sense, probably, to throw off one more pawn to revive the c7-bishop: 22...e4!? 23.♕xe4 ♗g6, creating a certain counterplay.

23.♘e4!
Having regained the initiative, Anish began to play with inspiration. He considered that the most important thing was to contain the c7-bishop, and for this he does not feel sorry for a piece.

23...bxc5 24.bxc5 ♘f6
Black is unlikely to save himself after 24...♘b8 25.♕b2 ♔d7 26.♘bd2 ♔e7 27.♘c4.

25.♘d6+! ♗xd6 26.cxd6 ♖xd6 27.d4 c5 The king cannot run far: 27...♔d8 28.♘a5 ♔e8 29.dxe5 ♖e6 30.♕xa6 with a rout.
28.♘xc5 ♖e8 29.♕c4
Black resigned.

Standings after Round 11:
1. Nepomniachtchi 7 points, 2. Giri 6½, 3. Caruana 6.

Bloodshed, bloodshed!
Round 12 was the most combative round of the entire Candidates Tournament – all four games ended in victory for one of the sides! The finish line is rapidly approaching, so there is no time to be careful, it's time to lay out all the trump cards on the table. And, of course, accumulated fatigue kicks in: the resistance to defending worse positions has noticeably decreased.

The leader's closest pursuers met among themselves, and this was a clear case when a draw did not suit either of them.

NOTES BY
Anish Giri

Fabiano Caruana
Anish Giri
Yekaterinburg 2021 (12)
Sicilian Defence, Four Knights Variation

1.e4 Fabiano Caruana has a very versatile opening repertoire and he has many deadly weapons, but his 1.e4 is perhaps still the most feared one.
1...c5 2.♘f3 e6
I was hoping this would come as a minor surprise, as earlier in the event I had played 2...♘c6 and in general I have played a lot of 2...d6 lately, intending the Najdorf. That said, I certainly expected Fabiano to have something prepared everywhere, so the surprise value should also not be overestimated.
3.d4 cxd4 4.♘xd4 ♘f6 5.♘c3 ♘c6

The Four Knights Sicilian has been around forever and sometimes gets trendy at random points in time. The critical variation begins with 6.♘xc6 bxc6 7.e5, but not all players feel like getting into that mess.
6.a3!?
With this move White usually hopes to shift the focus of the game on to the middlegame. White prevents ...♗b4, but Black usually gets a fine version of the Scheveningen, with White having played a3 rather early. It is a useful move, but perhaps not always the main priority.
6...♗e7
Shakhriyar Mamedyarov played 6...♕c7 against Fabiano in the German Bundesliga last year.
7.♗e3 0-0 8.♗e2 d6 9.♕d3!?
An interesting move, adding a modern twist to the 6.a3 system. Previously, you would expect players to castle short automatically.

9...♗d7!?
As 9.♕d3 is one of the engine's top moves. I had seen it before as well and thought that this could be clever.

I remembered some vague, messy lines after this move and was hoping that Fabiano would remember them at least equally vaguely

10.f4 Natural, as castling queenside allows ...♘e5, which leads to different complications.

10...e5!?
I remembered some vague, messy lines after this move and was hoping that Fabiano would remember them at least equally vaguely.

11.♘xc6 bxc6

12.0-0
Instead, 12.0-0-0 is met by 12...♘g4, but 12.♖f1!? deserves attention. The move Fabiano chose looks very harmless, but I realized there was some venom to it.

12...exf4
I also considered 12...a5, followed by ...♗c8, with the idea of ...♗a6, but finally decided to go for the natural response. That obsession to plant the knight on e5 must be the trauma I ended up with after all that Najdorf lately.

13.♗xf4

13...♗e6?!
I slightly misjudged things here, and the standard Najdorf idea of ...♗e6 and ...♘d7 and rerouting the knight to e5 is going to take quite some effort to implement.

As Fabiano Caruana pressed, desperately needing a win, Anish Giri defended patiently and struck mercilessly when his time came.

It felt as if 13...♘g4 should equalize too, but after 14.♗xd6 ♕b6+ 15.♔h1 ♗xd6 16.♕xd6 ♖ad8 even the simple capture on g4, followed by ♕g3, seemed not a hundred percent fine to me, and it also felt a little sad to play such a one-sided position.

It is interesting why 13...♘g4! is so strong, because at first, one might argue that Black's light-squared bishop is the better one of the two. That in itself being true, I think there may be other factors at play here. In some ways, Black has less space, and the bishop on e6 is potentially blocking my rook's view of the e-file. Also, White has to deal with some concrete issues like ...♕b6+ or ...d5 at the right moment. But perhaps above all it is because there is no other way to reroute the knight to e5 comfortably. 14.♔h1 (there are alternatives, but this is the most natural one) 14...♗xe2 15.♕xe2 (after 15.♘xe2, 15...d5! 16.e5 ♘e4 solves the opening problems) 15...♖e8 intending (if allowed) ...♗f8 and ...♖e6, pressuring the e4-pawn and at the same time neutralizing White's potential

pressure along the f-file, which would be a good demonstration of why it can be nice to get rid of the light-squared bishops.

14.♕g3!

The queen is well placed here, still hitting the d6-pawn and also with some ♗h6 in mind, at the right moment.

14...♘d7 I was really only choosing between ...♘d7-e5 and ...d6-d5 ideas, and as I felt the second one to be far too unattractive (with ♖ad1 and ♗e5 and all coming) I didn't hesitate too long here.

However, 14...h5! is the engine's top choice, with the idea to chase the

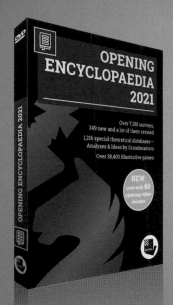
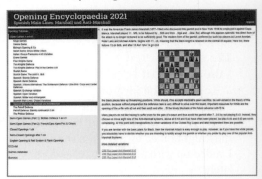

queen away from its ideal position on g3 and then eventually hit the centre with ...d5. I have to say it really didn't occur to me, especially as one would think that pushing kingside pawns and further softening the king's shelter is counterintuitive.

15.♖ad1!
Stronger than the natural 15.♔h1, when Black would be able to establish the knight on e5 directly. It turns out that ...♕b6+–xb2 is not a real threat.

15...♖e8 A fine waiting move. There was no easy way to get the knight to e5 and I had to watch out for ♗h6. Alternatively, I was considering 15...♔h8!?, and it is still hard for me to say which move was better.
15...♕b6+ made some sense, but not with the idea of capturing the b2-pawn: 16.♗e3! ♕xb2? (there is something to be said for 16...♕d8!, when the bishop on e3 is worse placed than on f4, but I am not this deep) 17.♘d5! (this is bad news) 17...cxd5 18.♗d4, and White wins the queen.

16.♔h1 ♕b8!?
I disliked 16...♕b6, as after 17.b4 ♘e5 White gets 18.♘a4 with tempo, but objectively it is not clear which move was better.

17.b4?! It seems that this wasn't as good as we both initially thought it was. White could have played it slowly with 17.b3!. His only issue is the knight on c3, which is dominated by the c6-pawn (a common theme in many early middlegame positions). Fabiano decided to solve that issue by removing the c6-pawn altogether, but there was an alternative way: 17...♘e5 18.♗h5!. Very strong. The bishop attacks nothing, but is merely freeing the e2-square for the knight. On d4, the knight will stand a lot better. Black is lacking a clear plan. The problem is, it is hard to further improve the pieces, and it's unclear how to really make use of the pretty knight on e5.

17...♘e5 18.b5

Clearing the way for the c3-knight.

18...♖c8!
Much stronger than taking the pawn and allowing the ♘xb5-♘d4 rerouting.

19.bxc6 ♖xc6
The rook is doing a great job putting pressure on the open c-file. White has cleared the path for the knight, but in the process has created a couple more isolated pawns, which may backfire...

20.♘d5 ♕f8!

Fabiano was in a very tough spot, given the tournament standings, and I should be the last person to criticize him here, as I made the same mistake in the very next round

I was very happy with this move, but actually, the simple 20...♗f8 was also excellent. Black is out of danger and White has a tough choice. Is he going to play ambitiously, at the risk of over-pressing? And what for?

21.c3
Playing for a win in a very passive way. Fabiano was in a very tough spot, given the tournament standings, and I should be the last person to criticize him here, as I made the same mistake in the very next round. In some positions, playing for a win is basically playing for a loss. But probably you still have to try. I don't know.
In hindsight, it would have been best for White to go 21.c4!, just to force a draw here: 21...♘xc4 (Black can't play for more either) 22.♗xc4 ♖xc4 23.♘xe7+ ♕xe7 24.♗xd6 ♕e8 25.♗e5 ♕f8 26.♗d6, with move repetition.

21...♖ac8 22.♖c1 ♘g6!?
My first instinct was to take on d5 and play ...♖c5, which was fine, but this move seemed very interesting as well, asking White more questions.

Alexander Grischuk undergoes part of the daily ritual. In the new normal the players were both searched and their temperature was measured.

hard to decide, since both options seemed good. But I didn't worry too much about it. I felt I couldn't go wrong at this point, since Black would be better either way.

29.♖cd1

29.♘e3 was a better option, not allowing Black to clarify the situation further and keeping more pieces and a little more intrigue on the board.

29...♗xd5! I finally decided that it was time to start cashing in.

30.exd5 ♘f4!

Usually the knight is great at e5, but here I am going after the c4-pawn. A pretty knight is good, but an extra pawn... that's a whole different level.

31.♕f2 White gets to keep the pawn for now, but I had seen this coming.

31...♖8c7! Guarding all the pawns on the 7th rank.

32.♖d4 ♕e8!? A sophisticated move. I had calculated a long line that seemed to win me the pawn.

33.♗f3

33...♖xc4!? This wasn't as winning as I had thought, but still a fine practical choice, since there was no obvious way to get anything more than what I got.

23.♗d2?! It was only after this move that I really felt things starting to turn around. I had expected 23.♗g4!? or 23.♗b5!?, when I didn't think White had crossed too many lines just yet.

23...♗h4!

The white queen doesn't have a comfortable square, and now there's also the idea of trading the dark-squared bishops.

24.♕e3?! White is placing too many pieces on the c1-h6 diagonal, setting himself up for a trade of the dark-squared bishops that is going to be a positional disaster.

24.♕d3! was better, running away from the trade: 24...h6 25.♖b1 ♗g5

26.♗e1. White is still very passive, but at least he keeps the good bishop.

24...♖c5 25.c4 h6!

Now the bishop trade is inevitable and the situation clarifies. White is facing a very depressing task. He has to sit and wait passively, hoping his position won't collapse.

26.♕b3 ♗g5 27.♗xg5 hxg5

The doubled g-pawns are nice. The pawn on g7 is guarding the king and the f6-square, while the g5-pawn is protecting the f4-square and can be pushed forward without compromising the king's safety.

28.♕g3 ♕d8 For a while now, I had been considering taking on d5. It was

34.♖xc4 ♖xc4 35.♕xa7 ♖a4

I had calculated ♕c7/b6 here, and then the ...♖xa3, ♕xd6 ♖xf3! trick worked. Strangely, Fabiano comes up with the h4 idea, which is something I had not seen at all. But he does so in the wrong position.

36.♕f2? White can't defend such an ugly position passively. Besides being a pawn down, he also has a bad bishop vs. a good knight, a weaker king, and what not.

Instead of the text-move, 36.♕c7! would have offered White chances to hang on: 36...♖xa3. Now 37.♕xd6 ♖xf3!, followed by an invasion with ...♕e2, is winning, but White has a strong intermezzo: 37.h4!. Defending against ... ♖xf3. Black is still much better, of course, but there is no win: 37...♘g6 38.hxg5 ♖a4. This is quite nasty, but White can resist: 39.g3! ♘e5, and White has a tough task ahead, but the game goes on with fairly limited material – only three pawns each.

36...♖xa3 37.h4 ♕e5!

Centralization. White is lost.
38.hxg5 ♕xg5 39.♖e1 ♖a8 40.♗e4 ♖a2

An amusing 40th-move moment. I thought this was a clincher, but after Fabiano finds the only defence, which I had missed, I have to go back. Fortunately, nothing got ruined, as my advantage is far too overwhelming for a tempo or two to really matter.
41.♖b1 ♖a8 42.♖e1
Giving me a second chance; but now with a little more time and a fresh look, finding a forced win wasn't hard.
42...f5
The slow 42...g6 or 42...♘h5 would have won easily as well.
43.♗b1 ♔f7
The threat of ...♖h8+ is unstoppable.
44.♖e3 ♖h8+ 45.♔g1 ♘xg2

White resigned.
In case of 46.♖g3 there is 46...♕c1+, followed by ...♕h1 mate.
A pleasant victory, and an important one as well. At least, it could have been.

∎ ∎ ∎

With this third victory (in the second half), Giri briefly broke into clear first place. But Nepomniachtchi's game was still going on...

NOTES BY
Ian Nepomniachtchi

Wang Hao
Ian Nepomniachtchi
Yekaterinburg 2021 (12)
French Defence, Exchange Variation

1.e4 e5 2.♘f3 ♘f6
In the first half of the Candidates tournament, the Petroff or Russian Defence also featured in my game against Wang Hao, but then I found myself on the other side of the barricades almost for the first time. This fire-resistant opening, the favourite

However, as one of my favourite sayings goes, 'it turned out pretty well'

choice of the majority of Chinese chess players, correspond to their 'safety first' strategy. However, if I had known in advance how difficult the tournament would be for the Chinese grandmaster, then, quite possibly, I would have chosen a more combative continuation. However, as one of my favourite sayings goes, 'it turned out pretty well.'
3.♘xe5 d6 4.♘f3 ♘xe4 5.d3

This is how Alexander Grischuk played against Hao a year ago. The transition to a French Exchange Variation is one of the latest trends in opening fashion.
5...♘f6 6.d4 d5

You can probably also play 6...g6 and 6...♗e7, but in my opinion, there is no compelling reason for Black to abandon complete symmetry.

7.♘d3 ♗d6 8.♕e2+

8...♕e7

The above game saw 8...♗e6 9.♘g5 ♕e7 10.♘xe6 fxe6 11.c3 c5 12.♘d2 ♘c6 13.♘f3 0-0 14.0-0 cxd4 15.cxd4 e5 16.dxe5 ♘xe5 17.♘xe5 ♕xe5 18.♕xe5 ♗xe5, and Black defended a not very pleasant endgame (Grischuk-Wang Hao, Yekaterinburg 2020, ½-½, 49).

8...♗e7 is another strong move. The loss of tempo is partially compensated for by the slightly awkward position of the white queen on e2.

9.♕xe7+ ♔xe7

9...♗xe7 10.♗f4 c6 is undoubtedly fine, but still too passive.

10.0-0 ♘c6

A move that Jan-Krzysztof Duda has recently started using. The idea is to force White to play c3, after which the knight will move to e7, after which, by playing ...♗f5, Black will solve all problems.

11.c3

A curious move order that confused

me. As a rule, White starts with a check: 11.♖e1+ ♔f8 12.c3 h6 13.♘e5 ♘e7 14.♘d2 ♗f5, with approximate equality in Vachier-Lagrave-Duda, Skilling Open 2020 (1-0, 44).

11...h6?!

More precise is 11...♖e8, when after 12.♘h4 g6 13.♗g5 h6! 14.♗xh6 ♗xh2+ 15.♔xh2 ♘g4+ Black's opening problems have been solved.

12.♘h4!

Having saved on the check, White has time to gain the advantage of the two bishops, and the course of the game should obviously favour him.

12...♖e8 13.♘f5+ ♗xf5 14.♗xf5 ♔f8 15.g3

Black is facing a fundamental choice. Until White has reached an optimal alignment, he can try to push ...c5, and the problem of the isolated pawn will be solved by ...d4 or compensated for by the activity of his pieces (but this is not certain). The second option is to believe in the general drawing tendencies and remember the statement of another Wang, Wang Yue: 'Chess is draw', be patient and stand.

15...♘e7 16.♗h3

16...♘c8

After 16.♗d3, I would probably have played ...c5. But I liked this version less: 16...c5 17.♘a3! cxd4 18.♘b5 ♗e5 19.cxd4 ♗b8 20.♖d1 a6 21.♘c3, when the bishop will go to g2, and only White will enjoy the game.

The computer suggests a strong and unusual idea: 16...g5, followed by ...♔g7, ...g4 and ...h5. Having seized space, Black puts the knight on f5 and gets a full-fledged game.

17.♘d2 a5 18.a4 c6 19.♖d1 h5 20.♘f1

The transfer of the knight to e3 with a further b3 and c4 seems to be a fairly logical plan. In any case, White has *carte blanche*, and he chooses an arrangement to his taste, while Black's ultimate dreams are to keep the compactness and coordination of his pieces and, at some point, pinch his surprised opponent with ...h4.

20...g6 21.f3?!

I did not understand this move. If White had won a tempo by driving the knight away, there would have been less to question, but without the urgent need to weaken the dark squares it was not worth it.

21...♘b6 22.b3 ♔g7 23.♔f2

at a repetition after 28.♗e3, but after any other white move I would feel rather stupid. And an attempt to push ...c5 in a more favourable situation could provoke my opponent into moving more than just the dark-squared bishop ☺.
28.dxc5 ♗xc5+ 29.♔g2 ♗b6
A reasonable prevention of b4.
30.♖ab1 ♖c6 31.b4

31...♘c7!?
Black had other moves as well, but I was hoping that Wang Hao would be ashamed of his light-squared bishop now.
32.♖xe8 ♘cxe8 33.bxa5 ♗xa5 34.♖xb7 ♘d6
Of course, the game has not gone beyond the bounds of approximate equality, but White's cornered bishop on the kingside gave me the moral right to play for a win. The straightforward 34...d4 35.c4! ♘d6 36.♖a7 would have led to a draw.

35.♖a7 35.♖e7 was also possible, since 35...d4 should not be feared: 36.cxd4 ♗xd2 (36...♖c2? 37.♖e2 ♘c4 38.♗h6+ drops the rook) 37.♘xd2 ♖c2 38.♖e2 ♘c4 39.a5 ♘xd2 40.a6 ♖a2 41.a7 ♔f8, with a draw.

As Wang Hao explains his emotional decision to resign the game, Ian Nepomniachtchi begins to realize that the Chinese's resignation has brought him very close to his goal.

23...♘bd7
As a result of White's help, the idea of 23...h4 has become more tempting, but I thought that starting active play with the knight still offside on b6 was premature.
24.♗g5
I was glad that Wang Hao wanted to exchange all pieces and offer a draw, but the next few moves puzzled me a lot.
24...♘f8 25.♖e1 ♘e6

26.♗e3
I was expecting something like 26.♗xe6 fxe6 27.♗xf6+ ♔xf6 28.f4 c5 29.dxc5 ♗xc5+ 30.♔g2 e5 31.♖ad1 ♖ad8, with a level position. On the

other hand, his unwillingness to part with all the bishops in one go is understandable. In addition, the bishop on e3 prevents the undermining of c5, so this has its own logic...
26...♖ac8 27.♗d2

In general, I had stopped understanding what was happening. In fact, this move is also quite understandable: the bishop defends c3, and on occasion it is ready to support b3-b4 or attack a5. But on the whole, humanly, the ♗c1-g5-e3-d2 manoeuvre looks outlandish.
27...c5
I considered 27...♖a8, to clearly hint

NEW IN CHESS bestsellers

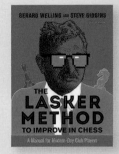
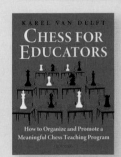

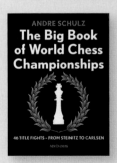
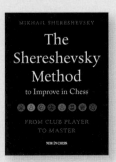

The winner of the 2020/21 Candidates with two of his most loyal supporters, his girlfriend Snezhana Fomicheva and his long-time coach Vladimir Potkin.

43...♔f6? But I should have been more careful deciding how to proceed. After 43...h4 44.g4 ♘d6 45.♖d7 ♘b5 46.a6 (after 46.♖d5 there is always 46...♘c3) 46...♔f6 47.f4 ♔e6 I could have readied myself to go for dinner.
44.a6 h4

45.♖a8 The only move.
If 45.g4, Black has the winning 45...♘e3, because after the knight swap the black rook will find it hard to get to the e-file. But, as you know, chess is a tragedy of one tempo, and now there is no forced win.
45...h3 46.a7 ♔e7
The best chance. The planned mating attack, alas, has been cancelled: 46...♖g2+ 47.♔h1 ♘e3 48.♖h8! ♘d1 49.♖xh3 ♖a2 50.♖h4 d3 51.♔g1 ♖xa7 52.♖d4, and draws.

47.g4 The computer assures us that there is nothing to worry about at all: 47.♘d2 ♘e3 48.♘e4 d3 49.♘d2 'Sitting quietly on the river bank...' 49...g5 50.g4 ♘d5 51.♔f1 ♘c7 52.♖b8 ♖xa7 53.♖b3... and you will see how your opponent offers a draw.
47...♘d6 48.♖b8 ♖xa7 49.♖b4 d3!? An attempt to play for domination. After 49...♖a2 50.♖xd4 ♖g2+

35...♗xc3 36.♗d7
An important move, after which White should draw.

36...♘xd7
Interesting was 36...♖c4, with the idea of 37.♖a6 ♘de4! 38.fxe4 ♗xd2 39.♔b5 ♖c2 40.exd5 ♗b4+ 41.♔h1 ♘xd5, and Black has the initiative.
37.♗xc3+ ♖xc3 38.♖xd7 ♖c6

39.♖e7? Optically, Black's position is a little more pleasant because a check from c2 is threatening and the king is about to arrive on e6, but any consolidating move will lead to equality, e.g. 39.♘e3 d4 (at the press conference we agreed that 39...♔f6? was strong, but after 40.♖c7! Black will have to fight for a draw) 40.♘d5 ♖c2+ 41.♔h3 ♘c4 42.♘f4 ♘e5 43.♘e6+! ♔f6 44.♘xd4, with a draw.
39...♖c2+ 40.♔g1 d4 41.♖d7 ♘f5 42.a5 ♖a2

43.♖a7? It was important to free the knight from captivity: 43.a6 ♖xa6 44.♘d2 ♖a1+ 45.♔f2 ♖a2 46.♔e2 ♔f6 47.♖b7, with excellent chances for a draw. I considered the move in the game almost suicidal, so I played pretty quickly.

51.♔h1 ♖f2 52.♔g1 ♖xf3 53.♘d2 ♖a3 54.♘e4! White reaches safety.

50.♖b3 I considered only 50.♖d4 ♖a2 51.♖xd3 ♘c4. The position is the same, but I still felt cheated.

50...♖a2 51.♖xd3 ♘c4

Of course, there is an almost forced draw on the board. Black does not really threaten anything, and this is the main problem and danger: the most practical solution – 52.f4 – is not strictly forced. Wang Hao is in no hurry with exchanges, but in the sixth hour of play, knights become especially jumpy and unpredictable.

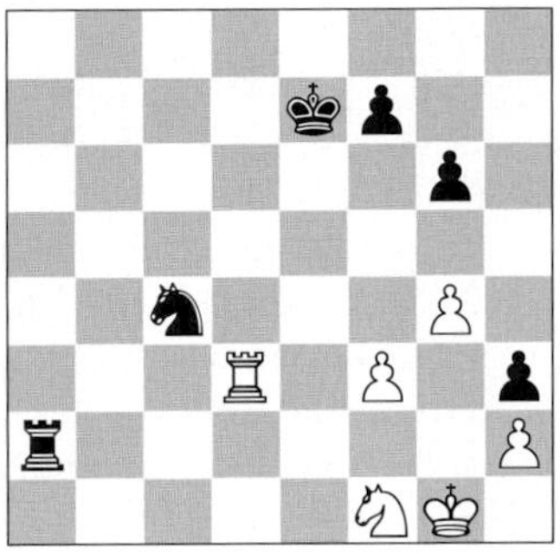

52.♘g3 Better was 52.f4! ♖g2+ 53.♔h1 ♖f2 54.♔g1 ♖xf4 55.♘e3, and with the knight swap the intrigue in the game fades away.

52...♖g2+ 53.♔h1

Sacrificing the pawn was practical in its own way: 53.♔f1 ♖xh2 54.♘e4 ♖a2 55.♔g1. Now White is no longer at risk of being mated, and there are probably no other ways to lose.

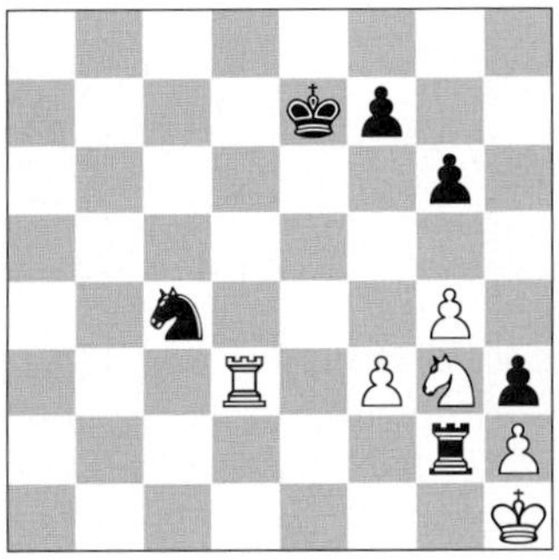

53...♔f8! A trap! But seriously, the check from e3 helps White out in many variations, so it is better to neutralize it.

53...♖d2 looks dangerous for White,

Suddenly the prospect of an exciting final round went out of the window

but in reality it is an easy draw. Taking this opportunity to instruct my young (and not so young) readers, I will give an example of a drawing fortress, the knowledge of which may be useful: 54.♖xd2 ♘xd2 55.f4 ♔e6 56.♘e2 ♘e4 57.♔g1 f5 58.gxf5+ gxf5 59.♘d4+ ♔f6 60.♘xf5 ♔xf5 61.♔f1 ♔xf4

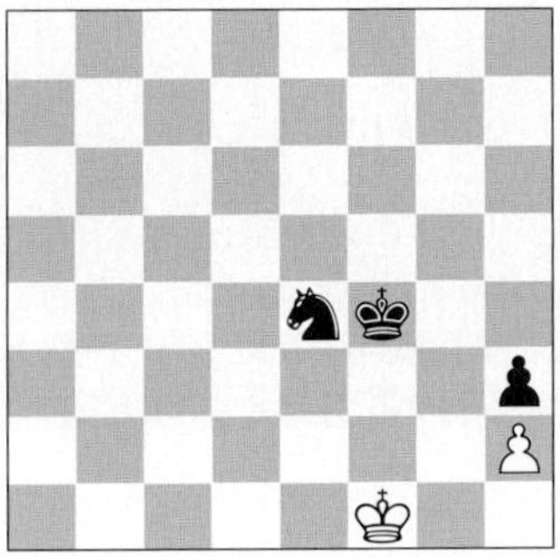

ANALYSIS DIAGRAM

62.♔g1 ♔f3 63.♔h1 and it's a draw.

54.♖c3? The desire to make a tempo move to prevent his opponent from strengthening the position brings White down. The right move was 54.g5, fixing the pawns on the kingside.

54...♘b2

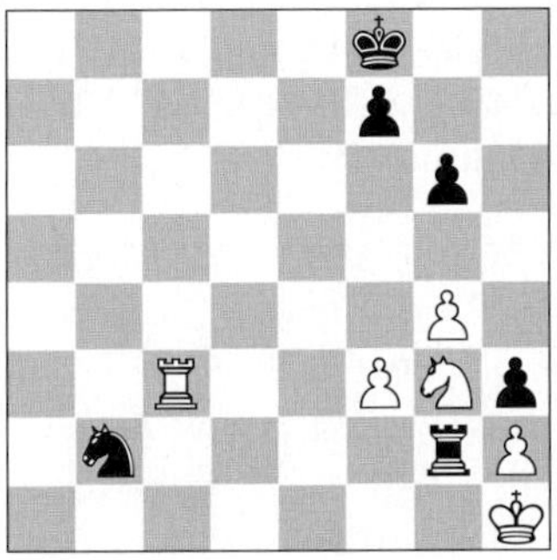

When, after a stubborn defence in a long and joyless game, you make an inaccuracy, and your opponent, rubbing his hands, prepares to checkmate in two moves, things become uncomfortable.

55.♖c8+ ♔g7 56.♖d8 ♖f2 57.♔g1 ♖xf3 58.♘e4 ♖e3

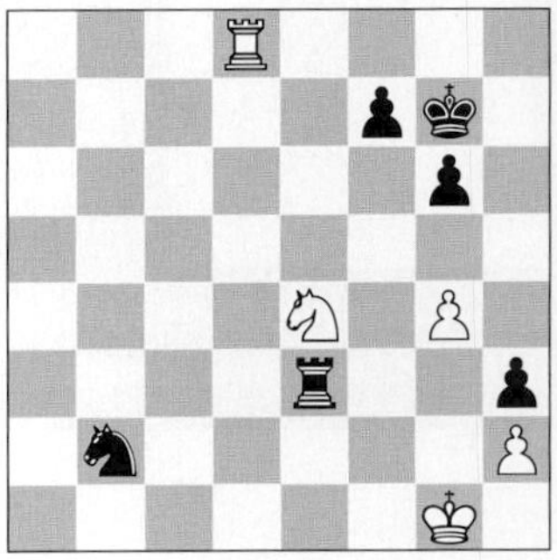

59.♘g3? To be honest, my position was improving so rapidly that I considered it almost won, so I was surprised by the computer estimate after the strongest 59.♘d6!. For example, 59...♘d3 60.♖e8 ♖f3 61.g5 ♘f4 62.♖e7 ♘d5 63.♖e1, and with moderately accurate play White should hold. It seems that Wang Hao was completely upset, having lost a pawn on f3, and felt the same as me, although his position became hopeless only after the knight's passive retreat.

59...♖a3!

It's never too late to blunder: 59...♘d3 60.♘f1 ♖f3 61.♘d2 with a repetition, so I was happy to move the rook away from various attacks.

Yekaterinburg 2020/2021

			1	2	3	4	5	6	7	8		TPR
1 Nepomniachtchi	RUS	2789	**	0 ½	1 ½	½ ½	1 0	½ ½	½ 1	1 1	8½	2849
2 Vachier-Lagrave	FRA	2758	1 ½	**	½ ½	½ 0	1 ½	½ 0	½ 1	½ 1	8	2823
3 Giri	NED	2776	0 ½	½ ½	**	½ 1	½ 1	½ 0	1 0	½ 1	7½	2800
4 Caruana	USA	2820	½ ½	½ 1	½ 0	**	0 ½	½ ½	1 ½	½ 1	7½	2793
5 Ding Liren	CHN	2791	0 1	0 ½	½ 0	1 ½	**	½ 1	½ 1	0 ½	7	2768
6 Grischuk	RUS	2777	½ ½	½ 1	½ 1	½ ½	½ 0	**	½ 0	½ ½	7	2770
7 Alekseenko	RUS	2696	½ 0	½ 0	0 1	0 ½	½ 0	½ 1	**	½ ½	5½	2702
8 Wang Hao	CHN	2763	0 0	½ 0	½ 0	½ 0	1 ½	½ ½	½ ½	**	5	2670

Here Hao gave up. Of course, this was an emotional decision, but at this particular moment it cannot be called unfounded and premature. Even a cursory analysis shows that the g4-pawn is doomed, and that there-fore, White's position is indefensible. Let's consider some sample lines:

60.♖e8 (the most stubborn. After 60.♔f2 ♘d3+ 61.♔e3 ♘c5+ 62.♔f2 ♘e6 63.♖d2 ♖a4 Black wins a second pawn) 60...f6 (Black is gradually improving his position) 61.♖e1 ♖a2 62.♖e3 ♘c4 63.♖c3 ♖a1+ 64.♔f2 ♘e5 65.♘e4 ♘xg4+ 66.♔g3 ♖g1+ 67.♔xh3 f5

ANALYSIS DIAGRAM

and Black wins.
An exhausting game in which the play from both sides was far from perfect. Nevertheless, in the Candidates Tournament, the result is what counts, and this most important victory allowed me to reach +4 and maintain my lead over the raging Anish Giri.
Wang Hao is a wonderful chess player, and it is a pity that health problems did not allow him to show every-

Andrey Simanovsky, the owner of Sima-land, handed out the prizes. In a week's time MVL's dream was shattered while Ian Nepomniachtchi's dream came true.

thing he is capable of in the second half. I really hope that he will be able to overcome this difficult period, will not leave professional chess and will continue to delight us with his original and very strong game!

■ ■ ■

Standings after Round 12:
1. Nepomniachtchi 8 points, 2. Giri 7½, 3. Vachier-Lagrave 6½.

An early finish
In Round 13, the intrigue suddenly vanished. With two rounds to go and only half a point behind, Anish Giri looked like a serious threat to the leading Nepomniachtchi, especially given the great shape the Dutchman was in. But his proximity was slightly deceptive. In actual fact he was more than half a point behind. Simply catching up with his Russian rival would not suffice, as in case of a tie the rules worked against Giri: in that case their direct encounters would be the first tiebreaker and in the first round of the Candidates tournament, played some 400 days ago, Giri had lost to Nepomniachtchi...

And so, in Round 13, playing with the black pieces, Giri took unwar-ranted risks in a position where he should have aimed for a draw and was duly punished by Alexander Grischuk. The Russian could not be blamed for his win, of course, but showed little excitement when he was interviewed after the game. 'There is nothing to be proud of, I really feel like a terrorist.'
Suddenly the prospect of an exciting and nerve-wracking final round, as we had seen in the most recent Candidates tournaments, went out of the window. Nepomniachtchi, having made a draw with MVL, secured tournament victory with one round to spare.
And it didn't matter anymore that both he (against Ding Liren) and Giri (against Alekseenko) lost their games on the last day. Those games had become fairly meaning-less afterthoughts. The only thing that mattered was that Ian Nepom-niachtchi had earned the right to challenge Magnus Carlsen for the world title in Dubai coming November! ■

The day after his victory, Ian Nepomniachtchi visited Sima-land, sponsor of the Candidates and Russia's largest wholesale company, selling more than 600,000 different products for home, work and leisure.

Finding Nepo

Is Ian Nepomniachtchi ready for the biggest challenge in his career?

The date has been set, the players are known. In November, Russia's Ian Nepomniachtchi will challenge Magnus Carlsen in a 14-game match in Dubai for the world title. **MARK GLUKHOVSKY,** chess journalist and executive director of the Russian Chess Federation, weighs the chances of his compatriot to dethrone 'the strongest chess player of the 21st century'.

I wrote my first article about Ian Nepomniachtchi in 2003, almost 20 years ago, when I found myself at the Russian Youth Championship by chance. I did not follow the tournament intrigue, and attended only the last round, but luck was with me. I saw something that will be remembered for a long time. Already at the age of 12, Ian was making a strong impression. In fact, although still a child, he

was in the lead in the Russian Under-18 championship, easily and artistically getting the better of much older rivals. In the last round, Ian played against 18-year-old Igor Kurnosov, a serious young man from Chelyabinsk[1]. Ian played fast and strongly, in the style of the young Anand. Despite the fact that a draw was enough for overall victory, he played a risky variation of the French Defence as Black and outplayed his opponent. But he made a mistake in

an already winning position. Later, Igor Kurnosov would say that this victory strengthened his resolve to stay in chess, since this was his last chance in a youth competition. For 12-year-old Ian, who cried all evening in his coach's suite, there was no such

---

[1] Igor Kurnosov would become a strong grandmaster, win several tournaments and die tragically under the wheels of a car in his hometown. In Chelyabinsk, a strong Open is held annually in his honour.

question – whether or not to stay in chess – even then.

Ian is a popular figure with journalists, and the milestones in his biography are well known. He was born and raised in Bryansk, a provincial town 350 km from Moscow, in a teacher's family. His mom is a teacher of mathematics, his grandfather and uncle taught Russian and literature. Both grandfather and uncle wrote poetry. Ian does not follow in this tradition, but he knows Russian poetry well, and even wrote several talented epigrams that were widely circulated within the chess scene. Since childhood, Ian has read extensively, studied not only English, but also German, and at the age of 16 he graduated from school with a gold medal. For him, education has never been an unpleasant duty that only distracted him from tournaments. Ian grew up without a father, but his uncle and grandfather never left him without attention. They taught him to play chess when Ian was not yet five years old. He learned to play chess before he could read. It quickly became clear what tremendous talent lived inside the small, slender, nimble child. Soon he was taken under the wing of the strong

native Bryansk. These tournaments are held to this day.

Ian easily went through all the different youth categories, confidently becoming champion of Russia, Europe and the world U12 (having beaten Magnus Carlsen along the way). By 2003, in the episode in which my story began, he was simply planning to win the Russian U18 Championship, thus rounding off his achievements in youth chess.

From that moment, which coincided with growing up and the transition from child to youth, something in his sports career went wrong. His peers and already obvious competitors, Magnus Carlsen and Sergey Karjakin, quickly became grandmasters and began to shine in elite tournaments. Ian, who was in no way inferior, seemed to be lacking in nothing that might thwart his development: he had a loving family, strong coaches and regular sponsorship. However, his rating curve in that period less resembles a rocket trail than an electrocardiogram of his supporters.

Ian's long-time mentor and later close friend grandmaster Sergei Yanovsky recalls: 'In his youth, it

stages of the game, eagerly analysed any position, was happy to share information with his peers, and prepared with friends for games. But he was hampered by the lack of a professional approach: the unwillingness to make a quick draw here and there, take a break, look after himself. He played to the maximum, and his physical condition did not always allow him to do this. His energy was running out, and with it – his good results.'

At the age of 17, Ian confidently won the Aeroflot Open – it seemed that the crisis had been overcome. But literally within months he lost the extra rating points again and continued – until 2010 – to remain 'young, bright and promising'. During this time his rivals (all born in 1990!) had moved far ahead.

Ian himself later complained that his childhood successes had come to him too easily. Constant victories seemed natural, rare defeats accidental and ridiculous. With this approach, every failure left a sore wound in his soul. It took him years to learn how to cope with his nerves and respect his rivals. 2010 became a turning point, when Ian won the European Championship, became Russian Champion after a great fight with Karjakin, and played brilliantly on the first board of the second Russian team at the Olympiad in Khanty-Mansiysk. His rating crossed the psychologically important mark of 2700, and he began to play regularly for the Russian national team. In those team competitions he showed absolutely phenomenal results: from 91 games with the classical time-control he scored 63½ points (+ 42 -6 = 43), often on first board.

At the same time, he was also quickly becoming one of the best chess players in the world in fast formats: he won the famous Aeroflot blitz, and took prizes at the World Championships. However, the upward movement in classical tour-

For 12-year-old Ian, who cried all evening in his coach's suite, there was no such question – whether or not to stay in chess

Soviet master Valery Zilberstein. Ian recalls: 'He came to our home, across the entire city, and studied with me for an utterly symbolic fee. All my openings – the Najdorf, Grünfeld – come from him. He was a strong player, and not only in chess – he almost professionally played *preferans*, even earning money with it!' In 2005, Zilberstein passed away; six years later, having earned his first serious money in chess, Ian initiated a tournament in his memory in his

was difficult for Ian to tune in to a full-fledged game with his peers. He played brilliantly against opponents older and stronger than himself, and it seemed to him that he had to beat each and every one of them. A huge number of points, both tournament and rating, were lost precisely because of this approach, which Ian has long outlived now. As a strong, versatile chess player, he was formed very early: he brilliantly absorbed information, was interested in all naments remained rather slow: he got into the world top-10 only in 2019, and into the world top five in 2020. Until 2019, he had played unsuccessfully in the qualifying competitions of the championship cycle, until he won the Candidates Tournament in Yekaterinburg – the first one he took part in in his career.

DotA star

Speaking about our hero, it is impossible to ignore the hobby that almost put an end to his chess career. In the world of computer games, just like in chess, he quickly achieved notable successes. Ian loved DotA (Defense of the Ancients), one of the most popular computer games in the world, which is of a strategic nature. The game's fans still remember the famous player Frost Nova, whose highest achievement was victory at the ASUS Winter Cup in 2011.

Fortunately, ten years ago, the computer games industry was still lagging behind the chess industry (now it is far superior!), and the choice between the two games was made in favour of the older one. 'I've been playing chess since I was five, and e-sports – much less', Ian Nepomniachtchi explained in one of his interviews. It seems to me that this was more of a joke: I cannot believe that Ian was seriously faced with such a choice.

Nevertheless, 'Nepo' continues to be a well-known figure in the world of e-sports. He is invited to tournaments as a guest of honour, a commentator and even a stats man, that is, a specialist who is responsible for statistics during DotA broadcasts. And he accepts these invitations if time permits.

It seems to me that Ian's popularity among computer gamers slightly balances his chances in the virtual 'battle of the fans' for the upcoming World Championship match. Of course, Magnus Carlsen is much more of a popular media figure in the Western world, but fans of computer

Two years ago, Ian began to sport a short but warlike pigtail with a vaguely Buddhist look

games may prefer 'one of ours'. And this is a very significant and active social stratum on the Internet.

Respected representatives of the Soviet chess school have the right to condemn Ian for his 'hobby on the side'. According to them, chess is the most important thing in life, and those who want to realize their talent should direct all their efforts towards it. In exchange for nothing, ever! But I would not like to engage in moralizing in this article. Even in Soviet times, there were different World Champions: not only Botvinnik or Kasparov, but also the much more frivolous Tal and Spassky. There is no doubt that his fascination with computer games prevented Ian from showing his true abilities in chess earlier. But let's not forget that

each person has his own path, and a straight road does not always lead to the goal faster.

Similar matches

Two years ago, when Ian's results finally coincided with the enormous chess potential that had been inherent in him since birth, he began to sport a short but warlike pigtail with a vaguely Buddhist look. Does this accessory mean that Ian has finally embarked on the path prepared by fate? And how far can he walk on it? In an interview that I had with him in January of this year, several months before the start of the second half of the Candidates Tournament, he spoke very definitely. The goal was clear and simple: to win the Candidates Tournament and then the match.

His play in the second half of the Candidates showed that he had got rid of many of the problems that had accompanied him since his youth. Ian played extremely strong and confident chess. He clearly chose his targets (see his games against Alek-

In 2002 Ian Nepomniachtchi became U12 Junior World Champion in Crete, ahead of Magnus Carlsen (on the left Dmitry Andreikin, also born in 1990!).

NEW IN CHESS

Old friends at the closing ceremony of the 2011 Tal Memorial in Moscow. This time Magnus Carlsen won the trophy.

Champion is the clear favourite, surpassing the Challenger in almost all respects: fitness, match experience, tournament achievements. But the Challenger also has strengths – he is not afraid of the Champion and holds a positive score against him in games with a classical time control (+ 4 -1 = 6). Carlsen himself admits that Nepomniachtchi can outplay him, and such recognition is telling! To beat Kasparov, Kramnik had to give up his usual way of life and change a lot in himself. And to come up with an opening concept that changed chess for years to come. And also to form a team of people who worked for him. And to lose 15 kg and begin to exercise regularly. And to stop smoking. Goodness gracious, who are those people who plan to write their name in the history of chess in golden letters?

Whether Nepomniachtchi is capable of such a metamorphosis, we all find out very soon. Like you, my dear readers, I don't know how big Ian's chances are in a match against the strongest chess player of the 21st century. But I'm sure of something else. If there is a person in the world who can give Carlsen a run for his money, his name is Ian Nepomniachtchi. ∎

seenko and Wang Hao), did not take excessive risks against his rivals, and never put himself in danger of losing while going for early victory.

One year ago, in the first half of the Candidates, he played brilliantly – not surprising anyone, because everyone has long been accustomed to this. In the second half he played super-professionally – and this is already a new Ian, who, as it seems to me, changed a lot in himself during the year of the pandemic. The very fact that Ian did not 'burn out' this time is very indicative. Patience has never been his strong suit. There are still six months ahead, which may become decisive for his fate. In order to crush a titan like Carlsen, Ian will need a transformation similar to that of Vladimir Kramnik when he faced Garry Kasparov in London in 2000. It seems to me that a lot of parallels can be drawn between these two matches. The reigning World

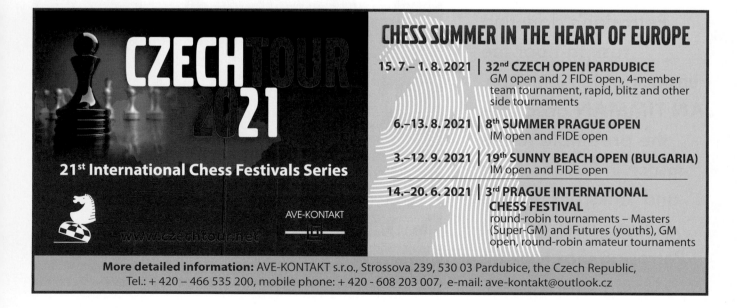

The Unstoppable American

Half a century ago, Bobby Fischer set a stunning record as he cleared his path to the title match with World Champion Boris Spassky. In the 1971 Interzonal, Fischer won his last six games. Next he trounced Taimanov and Larsen 6-0 in the Candidates matches. In the Final, it was Tigran Petrosian's daunting task to floor the unstoppable American. **JAN TIMMAN** describes the preamble to the match in Buenos Aires and looks at Fischer's first game against Petrosian that took his winning streak to 19.

How Bobby Fischer capped his phenomenal 19-game winning streak on the road to Reykjavik

The Soviets were worrying greatly, and had been doing so even before Bent Larsen lost the Candidates match in Denver 6-0, the same surreal score that had been Mark Taimanov's fate two months earlier. On 7 June, a 'Meeting of the USSR Chess Federation Coaches Council' was held in Moscow. This extensive appellation designated that officials and top players assembled to discuss the developments in the Candidates Matches. They were all there, including Spassky and Petrosian. Fischer was the central subject in the meeting. First of all, Taimanov's vicissitudes were discussed. Kotov got up to speak: 'During the match Fischer played tennis. He has coordination. He speaks four languages. He is an ideal chess player in every respect. Incredible concentration. A kind of harmony. He is forever carrying a pocket chess set or a chess book with him. His weird traits only manifest themselves during negotiations. He has a way of constantly repeating: when I become world champion I will

After his win in the first game, Bobby Fischer lost the second against Tigran Petrosian. Still, he won 6½-2½ in the end.

play three matches a year and not one match in three years.'

This was a somewhat incoherent argument, and I think Kotov must have had a few glasses of vodka already. But the message was clear: Fischer was a great threat to Soviet hegemony. Spassky reacted: 'When we have all lost to Fischer, will all of us be dragged on the carpet?' Upon which Petrosian replied: 'Yes, but not here.' You could taste the irony in these words, but still, they had the wind up!

The other semifinal match in Moscow, between Petrosian and Kortchnoi, had started with eight draws. At that moment Fischer had already won 6-0. Petrosian won the ninth game with white and held the last game to a draw, deciding the struggle in his favour. Soon, a rumour machine got going: it was alleged that the authorities had forced Kortchnoi to lose, since Petrosian would have better chances against Fischer. Not everybody believed this story. In an article in *Chess in Canada*, Larsen wrote: 'Many Americans believe the result of the Petrosian-Kortchnoi match was "arranged" because Russian officials consider Petrosian the most dangerous opponent for Fischer. This is incredible nonsense for me!'

However, Anatoly Karpov confirmed the story in the following words (quoted in the book *Russians vs Fischer* that was published in 1994): 'It was already clear that the winner would have to play Fischer, who was swiftly climbing another staircase to the chess throne. It seemed almost certain that Spassky would cope with him, but the Sports Committee decided that it would be better to prevent things from reaching that point and to stop Fischer at the approaches to a world championship match. So the officials summoned Petrosian and Kortchnoi, and asked them bluntly which of them had the better chances against Fischer. Kortchnoi said that in the "genera-

tion beaten by Fischer" practically no one had such chances. But Petrosian said he had faith in himself. After that Kortchnoi was told to lose to Petrosian. As compensation he was promised that he would be sent to three major international tournaments (a truly royal present to a Soviet chess player in those days).'

Karpov concluded his account as follows: 'Such is the story of what happened. Needless to say that there are no documents confirming this deal. But the quality of Kortchnoi's play – and most important of all, the fact that, having lost to Petrosian, he continued to maintain good relations with him, an amazing fact considering his character – confirm that there was no struggle. Kortchnoi simply stepped aside.'

What is striking in Karpov's argument is that he, as well as the Soviet authorities, had faith in Spassky and Petrosian: they would be able to stop Fischer. Kortchnoi's comment is interesting. In fact, he implied that Petrosian, who was six years older than Larsen, would have no chance against Fischer – and neither would he himself, who was yet four years older. What Karpov writes about the three promised tournaments is correct. Around the turn of the year, Kortchnoi played in the traditional Hastings tournament,

sharing the win with Karpov. In 1972, he competed in the IBM tournament in Amsterdam and in the great tournament in Palma de Mallorca.

In fact, Larsen agreed that Petrosian had the best chances against Fischer. He wrote: 'I consider the chances in that match about even, while I think

that Fischer could beat Kortchnoi who gets into time pressure too much.' In general, Fischer wasn't labelled as the odds-on favourite. Petrosian had beaten Botvinnik and Spassky in long matches. If he could

reach that level once again, he could be considered the slight favourite. On the other hand, Fischer had performed much better in the recent past. If we consider only the quarter-final and the semifinal, Petrosian's two won games contrasted sharply with Fischer's twelve victories.

Fischer's Magnificent 19

Palma de Mallorca Nov-Dec 1970

1	Fischer-Rubinetti	1-0
2	Uhlmann-Fischer	0-1
3	Fischer-Taimanov	1-0
4	Suttles-Fischer	0-1
5	Fischer-Mecking	1-0
6	Gligoric-Fischer	0-1

Vancouver May 1971

7	Taimanov-Fischer	0-1
8	Fischer-Taimanov	1-0
9	Taimanov-Fischer	0-1
10	Fischer-Taimanov	1-0
11	Taimanov-Fischer	0-1
12	Fischer-Taimanov	1-0

Denver July 1971

13	Larsen-Fischer	0-1
14	Fischer-Larsen	1-0
15	Larsen-Fischer	0-1
16	Fischer-Larsen	1-0
17	Larsen-Fischer	0-1
18	Fischer-Larsen	1-0

Buenos Aires September 1971

19	Fischer-Petrosian	1-0

'During the match Fischer played tennis. He has coordination. He speaks four languages. He is an ideal chess player in every respect'

At the time of Fischer's triumphal march through the New World, Argentine grandmaster Miguel Quinteros was touring Europe, visiting one tournament after the other. After the match in Denver, he called Fischer to congratulate him. The latter's prompt reaction was, 'I want to play my match against Petrosian in Buenos Aires.' There was a time window of two months to organize this. Quinteros telephoned an official in the Argentinian Ministry of Sport who was a friend of his. In no time, a sum of $12,500 was transferred to FIDE. This is not a very unusual sum by today's standards, but it was unprecedentedly high in those days. The winner would receive $7500, the loser $4500; apparently $500 went to FIDE. With this, the Argentinians had outbid Belgrade, who had put in a bid for $10,000. The problem was that Petrosian absolutely didn't feel like playing in Argentina.

The two finalists negotiated over this pressing question via Svetozar Gligoric. From Belgrade, the Yugoslav grandmaster spoke by telephone with Fischer in English, and with

Fischer brought forward that the steaks in Argentina were excellent, which wasn't a very strong argument in itself

Petrosian in Russian, functioning as a go-between. Fischer brought forward that the steaks in Argentina were excellent, which wasn't a very strong argument in itself. The high prize fund was the issue. Fischer suggested that FIDE might go for the highest bid, upon which Petrosian replied that he couldn't be forced to play in Buenos Aires. It was a delicate situation. Naturally, Gligoric hoped that the match would go to Belgrade, but he

On his arrival in Buenos Aires, Bobby Fischer is received by a government official. On the right Ed Edmondson, Executive Director of the US Chess Federation.

COLLECTION DAVID DELUCIA

didn't make any hints about that in any way. Only later did it become known that Petrosian had wanted to play in Europe, but not in Belgrade. He had good reasons for this. He had never performed well in Yugoslavia, and his two defeats against Fischer from the previous year in the capital were still fresh in his memory. In addition, Fischer was extremely popular in Yugoslavia.

So where did Petrosian want to play? It seems that Athens was interested in the match, but it isn't clear whether the city put in any concrete bid. FIDE decided not to go for the highest bid; Euwe preferred to draw lots. Buenos Aires came out as the winner, which was good news for Fischer and Quinteros.

In preparation for the match, Fischer played a blitz tournament in New York, winning with the monster score of 21½ out of 22. He seemed to be ready for the big battle.

Orange juice and chorizo steaks

The Soviet delegation was the first to arrive in Buenos Aires. They had been under way for two days, following the curious route Moscow-Paris-Nice-Dakar and eventually reaching the Argentinian capital. Petrosian had Yury Averbakh and Alexey Suetin as his seconds. Petrosian's wife Rona was there too, while Viktor Baturinsky was the delegation leader. Baturinsky was the absolute top dog of Soviet chess. He was infamous for having been a prosecutor under Stalin. He was also a very strong player who had written a famous trilogy on Botvinnik. Later, he was also Karpov's delegation leader during the latter's matches against Kortchnoi.

Fischer arrived two days later, in the company of Ed Edmondson and Larry Evans, who acted as his second again. Quinteros collected them from the airport. He noticed that Fischer had a touch of flu and suggested postponing the match for a few days. Fischer would have nothing of this – illness could never be an excuse. This compelled Quinteros to compose a special diet for Fischer: fresh orange juice and chorizo steaks.

On 28 September, the day before the official opening, a press conference was held. It was attended by approximately 200 journalists from all corners of the world. One journalist asked Petrosian if the match would last the full twelve games. This was a provocation, suggesting that Fischer would again accomplish a series of victories. Petrosian's reaction was one of irritation: 'It might be possible that I win it earlier,' he said, adding, 'Fischer's wins do not impress me. He is a great player, but not a genius. I am glad to face him directly. I do not envy his triumphs and they cannot influence me, because I had many experiences of the same nature. I am not afraid of his aggressiveness. In chess, many factors play a role. Physically I feel excellent. I have prepared myself conscientiously for this match. I am confident that I will play accurately and well. For me chess is much more than just a sport. It has a relationship to intellectual development and art.'

This was a cunning expatiation that Petrosian must have carefully prepared – together with Baturinsky, probably. For Fischer too, now the moment had come to speak out clearly about his chances in the cycle. He said, 'I am the best player in the world, and I am here to prove it. I have waited ten years for this moment but I was hindered by Soviet manoeuvres. I shall depart from Buenos Aires before the 12th game is scheduled.'

A strong, courageous reaction. Whereas Petrosian had elaborated on his opponent's playing style, Fischer avoided mentioning names.

Baturinsky saw Fischer for the first time during the press conference. He struck up a conversation in Russian. The delegation leader was especially interested in Fischer's knowledge of Russian chess literature. And he was impressed by what he heard – Fischer knew a lot, and had read through almost all the available material.

The opening and the drawing of lots took place in the San Martin theatre, the same venue in which

the match would be played. Fischer arrived slightly late. He was handed a black pawn and a white pawn. The idea was that he would keep one pawn in each hand to allow Petrosian to choose the colour he would start with. However, Fischer had a problem with the procedure: he thought the pawns were too big. Petrosian might be able to see them through his fingers. A tad clumsily, Fischer held the pawns behind his back. Then, Petrosian tapped on his left shoulder – the black pawn was on that side. 'Fischer, clearly pleased, smiled,' comments Baturinsky. However, it wasn't clear if the drawing of lots had been so favourable for him. From my own experience, I know that it is not an advantage to start with white in a match.

Thousands of chess fans

Hours before the start of the first game, thousands of chess fans had already gathered in front of the San Martin theatre. The playing hall held only 1200 seats, and so the majority of the spectators gathered in the lobby, where Miguel Najdorf and Herman Pilnik would commentate on the games with the help of large demonstration boards.

In the first game, Petrosian managed to surprise Fischer in the opening. Then something unexpected happened: the lights went out. Petrosian later wrote: 'He (Fischer) paused for thought only after 14...0-0-0, became nervous and red spots appeared on his face. At that moment the lights went out. The

only light came from lamps in the side passages and from somewhere in the back. The board was, of course, visible, but not for normal playing. I got up. The arbiter stopped Fischer's clock, but he remained seated, staring at the position. Five minutes passed, then ten... I asked the interpreter over, and he called the chief arbiter (Lothar Schmid). I pointed out that Fischer ought to have left the table. But my opponent – the Fischer who had always put so much attention to the lighting – suddenly agreed to having his clock switched on and continued to sit at the table in semi-darkness.'

I do not quite understand why Petrosian thought that Fischer ought to have left the playing table. I would probably have remained seated at the board, too. Petrosian also relates that the lights went out again during the eighth game, at the moment when he had confronted Fischer with a novelty. He doesn't go so far as to suggest foul play. Of course, it was just a coincidence. Apparently, the meticulously laid on lighting system that Fischer had been insisting upon all the time was vulnerable.

I think that Fischer's reaction to the situation was better than Petrosian's. When you are confronted with an unexpected situation, it is important to maintain your concentration as much as possible. Why should you get up and walk into the semi-darkness, probably getting involved in conversations about irrelevant matters with others?

In any case, Fischer eventually managed to win the game.

Bobby Fischer (2760)
Tigran Petrosian (2640)
Buenos Aires Candidates 1971
(1st match game)
Sicilian Defence, Taimanov Variation

1.e4 c5 2.♘f3 e6 3.d4 cxd4 4.♘xd4 ♘c6 5.♘b5 d6 6.♗f4 e5 7.♗e3 ♘f6 8.♗g5 ♗e6 9.♘1c3 a6 10.♗xf6

Fischer stays true to his dubious variation, which almost backfired.

Hours before the start of the first game, thousands of chess fans had already gathered in front of the San Martin theatre

10...gxf6 11.♘a3

11...d5

For 11...♘d4, I refer to the 6th match game with Taimanov. The text move had not been seen in practice yet, but it had been recommended by the Latvian attacking player Alvis Vitolins in his comments on Fischer-Taimanov in *Shakhmaty Riga*. Petrosian knew about this – Fischer didn't.

12.exd5 ♗xa3 13.bxa3 ♕a5 14.♕d2 0-0-0

At this moment, the lights went out in the playing hall.

15.♗c4

It's strange but true: this logical developing move, protecting the d-pawn, is probably losing. White had two alternatives to keep his disadvantage within bounds. First, 15.♖d1, a developing move White will always have to make, to support the d-pawn. After 15...♔b8 16.♗c4, the situation is less alarming than in the game. There can follow 16...♘d4 17.0-0 ♗g4 18.f3 ♕c5 19.♔h1 ♗xf3 20.♗e2!, and White has reasonable chances to hold.

Probably, 15.♗d3 is White's best

Tigran Petrosian and Bobby Fischer wait for chief arbiter Lothar Schmid to start the game.

option, since this forces an endgame. After 15...♗xd5 16.♘xd5 ♕xd5 17.♗f5+ ♔c7 18.♕xd5 ♖xd5 19.♖d1, Black is better but White doesn't need to despair.

15...♖hg8!

There is a story to this move. After Petrosian had won his match against Kortchnoi, he was handed a sealed envelope at the chess club with 'For the winner of the match' written on it. Petrosian himself told the following about it: 'It turned out that in the analysis of the 6th match game Fischer-Taimanov, Candidate Master V. Chebanenko from Kishinev had found after 11...d5 12.exd5 ♗xa3 13.bxa3 ♕a5 14.♕d2 0-0-0 15.♗c4 the strong move 15...♖g8!. A careful check revealed that the Candidate Master had found an extremely important improvement...' A move in an envelope – as if it was an adjourned game! This account shows

how vulnerable Fischer's opening preparation could be sometimes.

16.♖d1

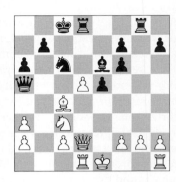

The only move, but Fischer must have played it with great reluctance. Now, Petrosian thought for more than half an hour.

16...♗f5

There has been a lot of speculation about the question why Petrosian didn't decide on 16...♗xg2. This logical capture gives Black a winning advantage. Petrosian himself wrote the following: 'Behind the board it sometimes happens that the opponent finds a refutation of a variation that has been invented at home, but in this case I had looked at exactly the move Fischer played, 16.♖d1, at home as well, and I had resolved to play 16...♗xg2 in reply – why I didn't play it, I cannot really say right away.' At the time, I investigated this position extensively in *Schaakbulletin* and I corrected and added a few things in *The Art of Chess Analysis*. Also in other publications, it received extensive attention. My new variations, widely branched, look like this:

A) 17.♕e3 ♘d4 18.♔f1,

ANALYSIS DIAGRAM

and now Black has the following options:

A1) The capture 18...♞xc2 was indicated by Kortchnoi and Furman in *64* at the time. It looks strong, but White has the saving move 19.♕d3!, e.g. 19...♜g4 20.dxe6! ♜xd3 21.♜xd3.

ANALYSIS DIAGRAM

At the time I assessed this position as favourable for White, but Kasparov has shown that Black can simply sacrifice his rook: 21...fxe6! 22.♗xe6+ ♚b8 23.♗xg4 e4 24.♗g3 h5. Black has the initiative and has excellent compensation, but White should be able to keep the balance;

A2) Already in 1971, I suggested the bishop move 18...♗g4, which has a deep point, as being winning. The main line runs as follows: 19.♚xg2 ♗f3+ 20.♚h3 ♕c7! (after 20...♗xh1 21.♜xh1 ♕c7 22.♞e4!, White can just maintain the equilibrium) 21.♜xd4 ♕d7+ 22.♚h4 ♕f5!, and White can prevent the threatened mate only with great material sacrifices. Kasparov – and the computer! – fully agree with this;

A3) 18...♞f5.

ANALYSIS DIAGRAM

This knight move too leads to a winning advantage. At the time, O'Kelly indicated that White could force a draw with 19.♕a7 ♕xc3 20.♗xa6. However, Black doesn't have to take the bishop. Kasparov has indicated that Black has a forced win: 20...♗xd5 21.♜xd5 ♜xf2+ 22.♚xf2 ♕xc2+ 23.♚f1 ♕b1+ 24.♚f2 ♕b2+, and eventually Black will take the rook, after which White is left empty-handed. This refutation of O'Kelly's variation is not difficult, but still I didn't mention it in *The Art of Chess Analysis*. With hindsight, I think that there was a psychological reason for this: unconsciously, I must have hoped that my move 18...♗g4 was the only path to the win.

B) 17.♞e4 is relatively best. Black can also make the bishop sortie to g4 now, but 17...♕b6! is even stronger.

ANALYSIS DIAGRAM

White's position is on the verge of collapse, as becomes clear after:

B1) 18.♕c3 ♗f5! 19.dxc6 ♜xd1+ 20.♚xd1 ♗xe4 21.cxb7+ ♚xb7 22.♗d3 (22.♜f1 is met by 22...♜xh2) 22...♗d5 23.♗c4 ♗c6, and Black wins with his mighty pawn front;

B2) 18.♕e3 ♞d4 (even stronger than the queen trade) 19.♚f1 ♗g4 20.♚xg2 ♗f3+ 21.♕xf3 (what else? After 21.♚h3 f5 22.♜xd4 ♗xh1 23.♜d2 ♕g6 24.♕g5 ♗xe4, White has nothing left to hope for) 21...♞xf3 22.♚xf3 f5 23.♞d2. Kortchnoi and Furman think that this position favours White. In reality, Black is winning. The queen is very strong, and also with his e- and f-pawns Black can unleash an attack against

the badly protected white king, e.g. 23...e4+ 24.♔e2 ♕d4 25.c3 ♕e5 26.♖he1 f4 and White has no satisfactory defence.

17.♗d3! The only move to maintain the balance.

17...♗xd3 Both Byrne and Kasparov give the push 17...e4 as being stronger. The computer considers both moves to be equivalent. After 18.♘xe4, Black can continue in two ways:

A) 18...♗xe4 19.dxc6 ♕e5 (indicated by me in *Schaakbulletin*) 20.♕e3 ♗xc6 (or 20...♕a5+ 21.♕d2) 21.♕xe5 fxe5 22.♖g1, and the endgame is equal;

B) 18...♕xd5 19.f3 ♗xe4 20.fxe4 ♕xa2 (or 20...♕c5 21.♕f2 ♕c3+ 22.♕d2, with a move repetition) 21.0-0 ♕xa3 22.♖xf6 ♘e5, and the position is balanced.

18.♕xd3 ♘d4 19.0-0 ♔b8

20.♔h1

Fischer prevents the capture on f3 and prepares to push his f-pawn. The alternative was 20.♘e4, when after 20...♕xd5 21.c3 ♕c6 22.♕e3 ♘e6, chances are roughly equal; both sides have a somewhat distorted structure.

20...♕xa3 Petrosian envisages

a transfer to an equal endgame. An alternative was 20...♖g6, to meet 21.f4 with 21...♖c8. If Black wanted to keep the tension, 20...f5 21.f4 f6 was possible. After 22.♖fe1 ♕c7 23.♖d2 h5, Black has slightly easier play.

21.f4

At the time, I gave 21.♘e4 as better. Kasparov doesn't agree with this and gives an '!' to the text move. Still, the knight move is certainly not worse, as after 21...♕xd3 22.♖xd3 ♘xc2, White has 23.♖f3!, with equal chances at least. He reserves the choice of how to take on f6.

21...♖c8 22.♘e4

22...♕xd3 Black didn't have to go for the queen swap right away. After 22...♕xa2 23.♖d2 ♖xc2, White would have had to exchange the queens after all. There could have followed 24.♖xc2 ♕xc2 25.♕xc2 ♘xc2 26.♘xf6, and now 26...e4! 27.♘xg8 e3 28.♔g1 e2 is the simplest path to a draw, as the knight ending doesn't offer White any prospects.

23.cxd3 ♖c2 24.♖d2 ♖xd2 25.♘xd2

25...f5 Surprising, but not bad. Curiously, Byrne even considered it to be

Black's only move. The computer sees things differently: the f-pawn push is its third move.

Black could also have maintained the balance by playing his rook to either g4, e8, d8 or c8, for example: 25...♖e8 26.♘e4 (the balance wouldn't have been broken either after 26.f5 ♖c8 27.♘e4 ♖xf5 28.♘xf6 ♘e3 29.♖e1 ♖c3) 26...exf4 27.♘xf6 ♖e2 28.h4 f3! 29.g4 ♖xa2 30.♘xh7 b5, and Black has sufficient counterplay.

26.fxe5 ♖e8 27.♖e1 ♘c2

That was the idea of Black's 25th move. To evade a move repetition, White's rook has to leave the e-file.

28.♖e2 ♘d4 29.♖e3 ♘c2

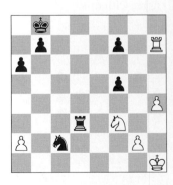

Here, Petrosian offered a draw. It seems to me that this can be explained as a sign of nervousness. Petrosian must have been anxiously hoping that Fischer wouldn't play for a win.

30.♖h3 Of course. Whenever Fischer saw a chance to continue the fight, he would do it.

30...♖xe5 31.♘f3 ♖xd5 32.♖xh7 ♖xd3 33.h4

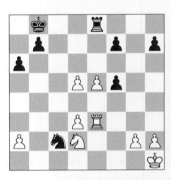

The passed h-pawn is potentially dangerous, but there is no reason for

Black to worry; his rook and knight work well together.

33...♘e3 Kortchnoi and Furman give a '?' to this knight move and give 33...♘d4 as the drawing move. This is indeed sufficient for a draw, e.g. 34.♔g5 f6 35.♘h3 ♘c6 36.♘f4 ♖d4, and White has achieved nothing. But in fact there is also nothing wrong with the text move; the knight strives for the vital square g4.

34.♖xf7 ♖d1+

Kortchnoi and Furman indicate 34...♔c8, to oppose on the d-file. Indeed, White does not have any winning chances in that case. On 35.h5, Black can stop the h-pawn with 35...♖d6, with the threat 36...♖h6. Suetin's recommendation 34...♖d6 is also good, e.g. 35.♔h2 ♖g6 36.♔h3 ♘xg2 37.♖xf5 ♘xh4 38.♘xh4 ♖g1, and White cannot maintain his a-pawn.

I indicated 34...b5, to set the queen-side majority in motion. The drawback of that move is that White can create tactical chances with 35.♘e5, since the c6-square is tender. 34...a5 is good. There are many roads to the draw; also the text move will do.

35.♔h2

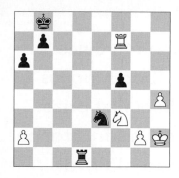

35...♖a1!

Another '?' from Kortchnoi and Furman, but in fact this is the only move to keep the balance, since it was too late for 35...♔c8, as now the white king decisively intervenes with 36.♔g3. After 36...♖d7 37.♖f8+ ♖d8 38.♖xd8+ ♔xd8 39.♘d4!, the knight ending is winning for White.

36.h5

Bobby Fischer draws a big crowd during a simul in the streets of Buenos Aires.

36...f4

Only this panic move in time-trouble is the decisive mistake. Black should have played the obvious 36...♖xa2. This way he keeps control of the g4-square, preventing White from pushing the h-pawn. White's best chance now is 37.♖g7, but it doesn't impress.

The most concrete drawing variation here is 37...♘g4+ 38.♔g3 a5 39.♘h4 ♖c2 40.♘xf5 ♘f6 41.♔h4 a4, and the black a-pawn provides enough counterweight.

37.♖xf4 ♖xa2 38.♖e4

Enclosing the knight. 38.♔h3 ♘xg2 39.♖f8+ was also sufficient.

38...♘xg2 39.♔g3 ♖a5 40.♘e5

Black resigned.

Fischer's nineteenth consecutive win! An unparalleled series that had started with his win against Jorge Rubinetti in Round 17 of the Interzonal in Palma de Mallorca. In fact, Rubinetti was the only player amongst Fischer's opponents who was not a grandmaster but an International Master. Still, he was a strong player, as testifies his win in the 1971 Absolute Argentinian Chess Championship.

Petrosian threw a spanner in the works in the second game that he won in grandiose style. Again, he managed to outplay Fischer in the opening, and this time he didn't let go. It wouldn't be enough to win the match. After three draws Fischer won the final four games, deciding the match 6½-2½ in his favour and earning the right to challenge World Champion Boris Spassky. ∎

This article is an excerpt from Jan Timman's new book **The Unstoppable American**: *Bobby Fischer's Road to Reykjavik (New In Chess 2021).*

Magnus Carlsen ends six-month drought

World Champion returns to winning as he tops New In Chess Classic

WINNER
WORLD CHESS CHAMPION
MAGNUS CARLSEN
$30,000 FIRST PRIZE

CHAMPIONSCHESSTOUR.COM

His last tournament win dated back to last October. Since winning Norway Chess and turning 30 in November, Magnus Carlsen had failed to do what he usually did: claim first prize. After months of discontent, the Norwegian shook off his frustration as he clinched the New In Chess Classic, beating old rival Hikaru Nakamura in the final. **SIMEN AGDESTEIN** reports.

Finally, after nine intense and stressful days – and let's not forget the four previous tournaments in the ongoing Meltwater Champions Chess Tour, where first place had eluded him – Magnus Carlsen could raise his hands in triumph, flash a broad smile and draw a big breath of relief. 'I'm just so happy! It feels really, really good.'

When he's competing on the chessboard, we occasionally see Magnus smile at some joke he's thinking of, and, perhaps more often, we see his temperament when he's done something stupid. But it's not often that we see him so utterly happy as he was after having beaten Hikaru Nakamura in the final of the New In Chess Classic. Even when he became

World Champion in 2013, he first seemed to linger on some inaccuracies in his last game instead of expressing his joy of having climbed the highest throne. Indeed, your focus should be on the process, and not on the results, as Arthur Kogan says in his Olalachess course, and I assume this approach is backed by all sports psychologists. This time, however, it was all about winning. Magnus left no doubt as to how much it meant to him. Obviously, a big burden had been lifted from his shoulders.

Magnus Carlsen is the World Champion and the best player on the planet, so something must be wrong if he doesn't win. That's the simple perspective. Yet, as every athlete operating at the highest level knows, the margins are small. If you look at the overall standings of the Champions Tour, he is in the lead, but his results include losses in two finals, both against Wesley So, and one third place. That is not enough.

Magnus has confessed that the weight of the World Champion title burdens him, but the perspective of not having it is even worse. Surely there are lots of interesting psychological aspects at play in this tour. The format with a cup waiting at the end of a long series of tournaments and the fast time-controls create lots of new challenges. Even your mouse-handling skills can be crucial, as So painfully experienced against Levon Aronian in the first game in the quarter final.

The position after 20.♖e3, as was So's intended move, is interesting, but

the rook accidentally slipped to e2 instead, and it was impossible to repair either the game or the result of the match.

Norwegian vs. Norwegians

Obviously, experience is of great importance for anyone striving to achieve something, but for many chess players the relevant practice has been hard to get in these pandemic times. The Champions Chess Tour and the Magnus Carlsen Tour of last year have been wonderful for those given the chance to take part. They were not only given a chance to win a lot of money, but also got the chance to compete against each other at the highest level. At the same time, a gap may have opened between 'the haves' and 'the have-nots'.

There are qualifiers to earn your place in the tour, but apart from this, the organizers have the option to invite players they find interesting for whatever reason. It's a tiny needle's eye the lesser gods can try to creep through, but it's surely better than nothing. Among the newcomers in 'the preliminaries' this time were two young Norwegians, Aryan Tari (21) and Johan-Sebastian Christiansen (22). With so few tournaments being held these days, it's not easy for young and ambitious players, but coming from the same country as the World Champion can be an advantage. I often can't help thinking of Johann Hjartarson's word of wisdom: 'Chess is a great hobby but a hard job'.

Aryan Tari became World Junior Champion in 2017, but has struggled to take the next step towards the elite. He got a chance in last year's Norway Chess, which wasn't a success, but did much better in Wijk

aan Zee this January. His score in the preliminaries of the New In Chess Classic was decent, 7 points out of 15. Although it was not enough to reach the knockout phase, it must have been a huge boost for his confidence. Hopefully he can bring that with him in the next Norway Chess coming September. For Johan-Sebastian this was the first test in a really tough field, and it was a sobering experience, as he only collected 1½ points.

I must admit that I paid special attention to the Norwegians and could not fail to notice the peculiar opening play by Magnus against

The weight of the World Champion title burdens him, but the perspective of not having it is even worse

his countrymen. As the World Champion, with tremendous knowledge of practically everything, and playing someone he really is expected to beat, he chose the following very slow set-up as Black against both of them:

1.e4 g6 2.d4 d6 3.♘c3 c6 4.f4 d5 5.e5 h5 6.♘f3 ♗g4

The argument is that the bishop stands better on f8 than on g7, meaning that Black has saved a tempo rather than lost one. It's not simple to win for Black here, but then this is how Magnus has beaten weaker players throughout his career, by simply going for a long game, trusting that his superior understanding eventually will pay off. We follow the games a few more moves:

7.♗e3

Against Johan-Sebastian Christiansen, Magnus was already better after 7.♗e2 e6 8.♗e3 ♘h6 9.♕d2 ♘f5 10.♗f2 ♘d7 11.a3 c5, although that game actually ended in a draw.

7...♘h6 8.h3 ♘f5 9.♗f2 ♗xf3 10.♕xf3 h4 11.♗d3 e6 12.0-0 ♗e7 13.♘e2 a5 14.a4 ♘a6 15.c3

15...♔f8 This was the game against Aryan Tari. I stop here, hinting at the knight manoeuvre ...♘a6-c7-e8-g7-h5, although action on the queenside is also possible. Objectively, White is fine here, but Magnus won in the end, although not without mistakes from both sides (0-1, 66).

The point is that practical play seems to be an essential element in this special format. Magnus is perhaps the foremost exponent of just that among the elite, but we see it also with the others who do well in these online tournaments. Playing skills are more important than opening skills, it seems.

Gawain Jones (33) is a bit older but still a newcomer in this type of tournament. He's already written two volumes on the Dragon, as well as other opening books, but looking at the score, this doesn't seem to have helped him much. Two draws was the meagre outcome of his eight Black games, and it wasn't much better as White, with a total of 3 points. The following game was surely interesting, though.

In a wild King's Indian, Gawain Jones got a winning position (much to the delight of his countryman Simon Williams), but the game remained highly complex and in the end Alireza Firouzja prevailed.

Alireza Firouzja
Gawain Jones
CCT New In Chess Classic 2021
(prelim-13)
King's Indian Defence, Classical Main Line

1.d4 ♘f6 2.c4 g6 3.♘c3 ♗g7 4.e4 d6 5.♘f3 0-0 6.♗e2 e5 7.0-0 ♘c6 8.d5 ♘e7 9.♘e1 ♘d7 10.♘d3 f5 11.f3

The beginning of a very interesting set-up apparently discovered by Firouzja. 11.♗d2 is the normal move here, the point being 11...♘f6 12.f3, and only now 12...f4, since ♗g4 is no longer possible.

11...f4 Black is supposedly happy to keep the knight on d7 for a while, delaying c4-c5.

12.b4 g5 13.c5

13...♘f6 Just a few weeks earlier, Radjabov had tried 13...♖f6 against Firouzja, but White could continue

his plan. After 14.a4 ♖g6 15.♔h1 a6 16.♖g1 ♘f6 17.♘f2 ♘h5 18.g3!? ♖h6 19.♔g2 White's king seemed safe, and Firouzja won in great style.

14.a4 ♔h8 The kind of stem game in this line was Firouzja-Aryan Chopra, Xingtai 2019. After 14...♘g6 15.a5 h5 16.♘f2 ♖f7 17.♔h1 ♗f8 18.c6 bxc6 19.dxc6 ♗e6 20.b5 ♘e7 21.♖g1 ♖g7 22.g3!? White succeeded with his active play on the kingside.

15.a5 ♖f7 16.♘f2 h5 17.♔h1 ♗f8

18.g3! Kudos to Firouzja for finding a completely new way of playing this classical opening. Viktor Kortchnoi did similar things – with a bishop on f2 – but it takes the same kind of guts and creativity to come up with a plan like this. One computer (perhaps not the best?) gives 18.a6 b6 19.c6, which to my understanding seems totally stupid and weakens my trust in its further assessments of these kinds of positions.

18...♘g6 19.c6 This is the essential set-up. White gets a majority on the queenside. **19...bxc6 20.dxc6 a6 21.♖g1 ♖g7**

22.gxf4

This defines the structure, but it was also possible to maintain the tension.

22...gxf4 23.b5

The thing about this set-up for White is that it's very easy to play. The plan is given, but not the move order. 23.♘d5 was also possible, of course.

23...axb5 24.♗xb5 ♘h7 25.♗d2 ♘g5 26.♘d5 ♘h4 27.♗e2

27...♗h3 This seems to have a tactical flaw, but what should Black do? White has lots of ways to improve his position, running with the a-pawn being the most obvious one.

28.♗c3?!

28.♗xf4! exf4 29.♘xf4 picks up at least three pawns, with dominance on the kingside. Instead, Firouzja calmly sacrifices an exchange for wonderful position play. But concrete tactics count for more here.

28...♗g2+ 29.♖xg2 ♘xg2 30.♕d3 30.♔xg2? ♘xe4+ 31.♔f1 ♘xf2 32.♔xf2 ♕h4+ loses instantly.
30...♘e6 31.♗f1 ♕h4 The problem is that Black can continue going forward with his pieces.
32.♕e2 ♘e3 33.♗h3 ♘g5! Jones is up to the job and plays brilliantly.
34.♗d7

34...♘xe4! The best, but note that 34...♘xd5 35.exd5 ♘xf3! also works, because 36.♕xf3 ♖g3 skewers the queen and bishop.
35.♘xe4 ♘xd5 36.♗e1 ♕d8 37.♗f2

Black is a pawn and an exchange up and is winning, but the position is tricky and, with very little time on

both clocks, Firouzja tricked his way to a full point.

37...♗e7 38.♗e6 ♘f6 39.a6 ♕e8 40.a7

40...♕xc6?

Apparently, 40...d5 gives Black a huge advantage, but now it was all about handling the clock. It's to be noted, though, that White still has the easier moves to find.

41.♖b1 ♘d7? 42.♕d3 ♕a4 43.♕d5

43...♖xa7?

43...c6 44.♗xd7 ♕xa7! 45.♗xc6 ♖b8 was the narrow path to keeping the game going. Seeing such things, which is quite inhuman, seems to be essential in modern chess practice.

44.♗xa7 ♕xa7 45.♗xd7

White suddenly is a piece up.

45...♗f8 46.♕e6 ♖xd7 47.♕xd7 ♕a2 48.♖g1 ♕e2 1-0.

Rameshbabu Praggnanandhaa (15) was the fourth and youngest of the newcomers. Perhaps he belongs to the category 'potential future World Championship contenders'. The pandemic may have delayed the young Indian's breakthrough, but

Annoyingly, in one round, three games ended almost instantly in identical fashion

hopefully his fantastic talent hasn't suffered too much. Praggnanandhaa scored a respectable seven points, but it wasn't enough to reach the knock-out rounds. Elsewhere in this issue, Jan Timman takes a look at his best efforts in the New In Chess Classic.

Irritating short draws

Several of 'the haves' – the established ones – seemed to regard the preliminaries, a 15-round round-robin spread over three days, as an obligatory walk they want to get through spending as little energy as possible. The only thing that matters is to finish among the first eight. This can lead to irritating short draws that are highly disappointing from the viewer's perspective. In one round, three games ended almost instantly in identical fashion after the following well-known moves.

1.e4 e5 2.♘f3 ♘c6 3.♗b5 ♘f6 4.0-0 ♘xe4 5.d4 ♘d6 6.dxe5 ♘xb5 7.a4 ♘bd4 8.♘xd4 ♘xd4 9.♕xd4 d5 10.exd6 ♕xd6

11.♕e4+ ♕e6 12.♕d4 ♕d6 13.♕e4+ ♕e6 14.♕d4 ♕d6 15.♕e4+ ♕e6 ½-½.

Hikaru Nakamura has a tremendous number of followers on Twitch, and he cannot be blamed for not entertaining his audience, but he also tops the statistics in this position. In total,

having had it both as White and as Black he has played it as many as 20 times.

Nakamura's route

The format sometimes dictates the way chess is played. In the quarter-final match against Le Quang Liem, Nakamura took the lead in Game 1 of the first match, and in the remainder it was all about surviving one wave after the other from the creative Vietnamese.

In the first game on the second day Nakamura really was on the ropes, but nevertheless prevailed. After this second win it sufficed for Nakamura to draw the remaining games to win the match.

The American's semi-final match against Shakhriyar Mamedyarov took a completely different course, with not a single draw in the ordinary match games. Nakamura won 3-1 on the first day, but on the second he lost 0-3. Eventually, Nakamura pulled the longest straw in the Armageddon tiebreaker. Opening-wise, the most interesting thing about this match was the discussion in the following line.

Shakhriyar Mamedyarov
Hikaru Nakamura
CCT New In Chess Classic 2021
(sf 3.2)
Nimzo-Indian Defence, Three Knights Variation

1.d4 ♘f6 2.c4 e6 3.♘c3 ♗b4 4.♘f3 0-0 5.♗g5 c5 6.♖c1 cxd4 7.♘xd4 h6 8.♗h4 d5 9.cxd5 g5 10.♗g3 ♕xd5 11.e3 ♕xa2

12.♗d3!?

Champion rating Champions

Among the highlights of the New In Chess Classic broadcast from Oslo were short videos in which Magnus Carlsen rated the World Champions starting from Bobby Fischer. He awarded them points (up to 10) for 'genius', 'entertainment', 'influence' and 'sanity'(!). Coming from a man speaking from wide experience and with a fabulous grasp of chess history, the verdicts are fascinating and perfect food for further discussions. And being a good sport, he even rated himself!

Bobby Fischer

Genius - 7: 'I don't consider him to be that big a genius, but still there was some Capablanca-like quality in the way that he made chess look very simple.'

Entertaining - 8: 'Everything about him was entertaining, also his games, because he always played for a win, even if they were not always exciting in terms of new ideas.'

Influence - 9: 'He scores very high both in terms of opening ideas and general ideas about the game. Everything around Fischer has influenced chess greatly.'

Sanity - 4: 'While he was World Champion he was still reasonably well-rounded. This is not a great score, but certainly later it could have been potentially even worse.'

Anatoly Karpov

Genius - 8: 'He has that Fischer and Capablanca kind of quality of making chess look simple. He was certainly extremely gifted, one of the most naturally talented players I have ever seen.'

Entertaining - 6: 'He was not that entertaining, he was more of the pragmatic kind of type.'

Influence - 8: 'Probably to a lesser degree than Fischer and Kasparov, but he certainly has influenced modern players and culture.'

Sanity - 7: 'There were some strange episodes in his World Championship matches, but I think in general Karpov has held up fine.'

Garry Kasparov

Genius - 10: 'In my opinion the greatest player there has ever been. Garry certainly was a very hard worker, but he had that very special talent for the game as well, that you could already see at a very early age. He could find ideas that nobody else could.'

Entertaining - 9: 'Generally everything about Garry was entertaining. He would have gotten a 10 except for his tendencies to offer a bit too many draws to my liking.'

Influence - 10: 'He really has influenced all the best players of today.'

Sanity - 7: 'There certainly have been episodes with Garry as well, but personally at least I found him very interesting to be around, not a problem at all.'

Vladimir Kramnik

Genius - 8: 'He was (as he is no longer active) extremely gifted.'

Entertaining - 8: 'There was a part in his career when he made a bit too many draws, but in his youth and in his last years his games were among the most entertaining to follow.'

Influence - 9: 'Kramnik has great influence on the new generation. He popularized the Berlin Defence and many other openings.'

Sanity - 8: 'Kramnik is relatively well-rounded, but he does have some interesting ideas.'

Vishy Anand

Genius - 9: 'Like Capablanca, someone who came out of nowhere. He was the first grandmaster from India, and has an unbelievable natural understanding of the game.'

Entertaining - 7: 'Anand definitely can be entertaining as a chess player and as a person, but he doesn't quite reach the level of some of the others.'

Influence - 8: 'It has been said that he was always the second person to play a good idea. He is extremely adaptable, but he wouldn't necessarily always come up with ideas himself. On the other had he has influenced an entire country to go from nobodies at chess to arguably the greatest chess country behind Russia.'

Sanity - 10: 'A perfect 10 for Anand.'

Magnus Carlsen

Genius - 8: 'I don't consider myself a genius in general. In chess terms I should score fairly highly, because I think I am quite naturally talented.'

Entertaining - 8: 'Obviously I am an extremely entertaining person, my jokes are drier than wood. I have some things going for me in terms of entertaining on the chessboard in that I am open to new ideas, I am always fighting towards the very end. But I also understand that my style is still slightly geared towards longer games and it's not everybody's cup of tea.'

Influence - 7: 'I am probably more on the Anand side here of not necessarily coming up with the ideas myself and being more of a follower than a creator. There has obviously been a bit of a chess boom in Norway, so that helps, but I think influence is not my greatest strength.'

Sanity - 9: 'I have my moments, good and bad. I am certainly one who can be upset after games. Usually it doesn't last, and there haven't been any too egregious moments so far. So the highest of these grades is going to be on sanity and it's going to be a very subjective 9.'

Magnus has played 12.♕c2 a couple of times. Understandably, Mamedyarov doesn't want to repeat that. Perhaps he won't simply sacrifice two pawns again either, if given another chance, but again and again and again, this is practical play, and confronting an unprepared opponent with surprises like this at least results in a lot of fun. It's not totally new, though. Considering the fact that Nakamura actually repeated the line in his two next Black games, it was clear that he wasn't totally taken by surprise.

12...♕xb2 13.0-0! White will regain the piece and hopes to exploit his lead in development and, of course, the weakened black kingside.

13...♗xc3 14.♖c2 ♕b4 15.♘b5 Threatening 16.♗d6.

15...e5 16.♖xc3

In the first game the next day, Mamedyarov tried 16.♘xc3, which is slaughtered by the computer, but soon the game reached calmer waters with a slight white advantage, and Mamedyarov winning in the end.

16...♘c6 17.f4 ♗g4 18.♕c2

18...♕e7

The first new move. Topalov-Ding, Wenzhou 2018, went 18...exf4 19.exf4 ♖ac8 20.♗c4 ♕c5+ 21.♔h1 ♕f5, and here White could have gained an advantage with 22.♘d6!. In Game 4 on the first day, Nakamura improved on this line with 19...♘d5, the point being 20.♖b3 ♘d4!. Mamedyarov calmly played 20.fxg5, but after 20...♘xc3 21.♘xc3 ♖ad8 22.♔h1 ♕d4 White didn't have enough to fuel his attack. 18...♘d5 has also been played a couple of times at top level.

The general feeling is that White doesn't have enough. It works the first time, and actually the third time, too, in this match, but it probably won't again.

19.fxe5 ♘h5 20.♗e1 a6 21.♘d4 ♘xe5 22.♖c7 ♕d6 23.♗h7+ ♔h8 24.♗f5

24...♘g7?

Obviously this is a hard position to defend with little time, but now it quickly goes downhill for Black.

25.♗g3 ♗h5 26.♕c3 ♖ae8

27.♘e6! The finish is elegant.

27...♖xe6 28.♗xe6 f6 29.♗xe5 fxe5 30.♖xf8+ ♕xf8 31.♕xe5

The game is over.

31...♔h7 32.♗f5+ ♗g6 33.g4 a5
1-0.

Carlsen's route

Magnus's way to the final was a bit similar. He played very solidly in the quarter final against Teimour Radjabov before things exploded in the semi-final against Levon Aronian. The only decisive game in the first match was the following one.

**NOTES BY
Peter Heine Nielsen**

**Magnus Carlsen
Teimour Radjabov**
CCT New In Chess Classic 2021
(qf 2.2)
Nimzo-Indian Defence, Classical Variation

**1.d4 ♘f6 2.c4 e6 3.♘c3 ♗b4
4.♕c2 d5 5.a3 ♗xc3+ 6.♕xc3**

6...c5!?

In an earlier game, Teimour Radjabov had played the more popular 6...0-0 against Wang Hao, a line that has become popular in recent years, since it allows Black to get close to equalizing. Here, however, he springs a surprise, having prepared a much sharper continuation.

7.dxc5 d4 8.♕c2!?

Perhaps 8.♕g3 could be seen as the more principled choice, but lately Black has been successful with 8...♘c6 9.♘f3 e5!?. White can indeed take on g7 or e5, but either capture would lead to interesting complications that Radjabov had undoubtedly prepared for.

8...e5 9.e3 ♘c6 10.b4 0-0

11.♘f3!

Exploiting the fact that 11...d3 can still be met by 12.♗xd3, because White controls the e4-square. 11.e4 a5! would have given Black far stronger counterplay than he got in the game, as the details favour Black. After 12.b5 ♘b8 13.a4 ♘bd7 14.♗a3 the point is 14...♕e7! when after 15.c6 ♘c5 16.cxb7 ♗xb7 17.♗d3 ♘fd7! Black has excellent counterplay. Since the rook is still on f8, ...f5 is looming, and the fact that White has lost a tempo compared to the game obviously helps Black's attack, too.

11...♖e8 12.e4!

Black's last move threatened 12...d3, followed by 13.♗xd3 e4, winning a piece.

12...a5 13.b5

13...♘e7

13...♘b8 is much worse here: 14.a4 ♘bd7 15.♗a3 ♕e7 16.c6 ♘c5 17.cxb7 ♗xb7 18.♗d3 is different from the above line, since the white knight is now on f3, and the black rook on e8. Both details obviously favour White.

14.a4 ♕c7 15.♗a3 ♘d7

Black's plan is becoming clear. He has stabilized the centre, and will now round up the c5-pawn. If he were

Among the highlights of the New In Chess Classic official broadcast were short videos with Magnus Carlsen rating World Champions or having his prodigious memory tested.

allowed to play 16...♘xc5, he would certainly have the better strategic setup.

16.c6! bxc6

With the queen on e7, Black had the ...♘c5 resource, but here the recapture is forced.

17.c5!

Black has won back the pawn and one can argue that he is ahead in development now. In addition, the a3-bishop is hemmed in by the c5-pawn. But as

Mihai Suba stated in one of his books, bad bishops protect good pawns, and with his next move, White will establish a protected passed pawn on b6, easily trumping all the above considerations.

17...♘f6 18.b6 ♕b7 19.♗c4 ♘g6 20.0-0 ♕d7

21.♘e1!

Nipping Black's counterplay in the bud. While both ♘e1 and ♗c1 are actually retreats, they are only of a temporary nature. Another concept of Suba's is at play here as well: White can keep on improving his position, whereas Black has reached his maximum without being able to improve further. Since he is unable to achieve anything, White has all the potential.

21...♗a6 22.♗xa6 ♖xa6 23.f3 ♘f4 24.♖d1 ♖aa8 25.♗c1 ♘6h5 26.g3 ♘g6 27.♘d3

The white strategy has triumphed. The black passed pawn has been blocked and is now more of a liability, whereas White's b6-passer, even though it isn't likely to queen any time soon, clearly has long-term potential, since any kind of endgame would be an easy win for White. In practice, this basically equates to having a material advantage.

27...♘f6 28.♗g5 h5 29.♗xf6 gxf6 30.f4

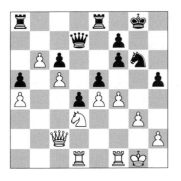

Black's counterplay is too slow. 30...h4 will be met by 31.f5, winning easily.

30...exf4 31.♘xf4 ♕g4 32.♖xd4 h4 33.♕d1! ♕g5 34.♕h5

Exchanging queens always favours White in view of the b6-pawn.

34...♕e5 35.♖d7 hxg3 36.hxg3 ♕xe4 37.♘xg6 ♕e3+ 38.♔h2

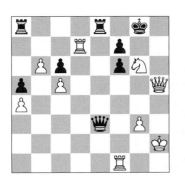

Having run out of checks, Black can choose between accepting instant mate and settling for the queen swap. Both are equally damaging.

38...♕e2+ 39.♕xe2 ♖xe2+ 40.♔h3 fxg6 41.♖xf6

And with c6 and g6 collapsing, Black resigned.

This game illustrates the tremendous power of the passed b-pawn. Although it seemed as if everything was happening on the kingside, it only did so while the b-pawn was dictating the terms of the struggle – without ever participating in it itself. That's real power!

■ ■ ■

I remember the first encounters between Magnus and Aronian very well. Apart from a blitz game in Reykjavik some months earlier, it started in Tripoli, Libya, in 2004. Magnus was only 13 and had been given a spot in the World Cup. He was set to meet the then experienced Armenian in the first match. After three draws Aronian finally won by showing brilliant endgame technique. Since then, they have met as many as 174 times. Magnus has won 59 times, Aronian 28. Magnus and Aronian know each other extremely well. Still, they manage to find new exciting lines almost every time they meet. Aronian started the creative show on move 5 in their first game.

Magnus and Aronian manage to find new exciting lines almost every time they meet

**Magnus Carlsen
Levon Aronian**
CCT New In Chess Classic 2021
(sf 3.1)
Italian Game, Giuoco Pianissimo

1.e4 e5 2.♘f3 ♘c6 3.♗c4 ♗c5 4.d3 d6 5.0-0

5...♕f6!?
Don't try this at home, as Magnus sometimes says. Breaking the basic principles of chess, such as going out with the queen early, is reserved only for the very best in the world.

6.c3 ♘ge7 7.b4 ♗b6 8.a4 a6 9.♗e3 ♗xe3 10.fxe3 ♕h6 11.♕e2 0-0 12.d4

12...g5!?
The centre is supposed to be locked before you storm on like this, but modern chess is all about what works in practice, as John Watson explained in his brilliant *Secrets of Modern Chess Strategy*. How well it works here can be argued, though.

13.♘bd2 g4 14.♘e1 ♔g7 15.♘d3 f5!?
Aronian continues his extremely active play.

16.exf5 ♗xf5 17.d5 ♗xd3 18.♕xd3

Even World Champions blunder… With 20.♗e2? Magnus Carlsen allowed Levon Aronian the nasty counterstrike 20…♘xd5!.

Impressively, Aronian managed to equal the score in the next game, drawing the first match 2-2.

Despite the general trend in these online tournaments to avoid sharp theoretical battles, new territories are explored, and soon become topics for theoretical discussion anyway. The following, from match day 2, was a follow-up of what had happened two days earlier in the match Firouzja-Mamedyarov and in a game Bluebaum-Giri just some weeks before.

Levon Aronian
Magnus Carlsen
CCT New In Chess Classic 2021
(sf 2.1)
Queen's Pawn Game: London System

1.d4 ♘f6 2.♘f3 d5 3.♗f4 ♗f5 4.c4 e6 5.♕b3 dxc4 6.♕xb7 ♗e4 7.♕xc7 ♗b4+ 8.♘bd2 ♕xc7 9.♗xc7

18…e4 Now it's suddenly about positional chess again. Black gets a wonderful knight in the centre for the price of a pawn. But 18…♘d8 19.♕e2! was horrible. **19.♕xe4 ♘e5**

20.♗e2? Even World Champions blunder. **20…♘xd5! 21.♕xd5 ♕xe3+ 22.♔h1 ♕xe2** And Aronian had succeeded fully, although he didn't manage to win the game.

Two games later it was Aronian's turn to blunder.

Magnus Carlsen
Levon Aronian
CCT New In Chess Classic 2021
(sf 3.3)

position after 42.♕d2

42…♕xd2+?? Aronian must have thought he was winning.
43.♔xd2 f6 44.♔c3 e5 45.fxe5 fxe5 46.♔b4

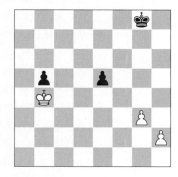

Now it dawned on Aronian that 46… e4 will be met by 47.♔c3, and the king takes care of both pawns. 1-0.

This strange position has occurred only three times, all of them in this year's Tour. Now Firouzja-Mamedyarov saw 9…♘bd7 10.e3 ♖c8 11.♗g3 ♗d5 12.a3 ♗a5 13.♖c1 ♔e7

14.♔d1? (it's strange, but the king

belongs on e2, as Magnus showed a couple of days later) 14...♘b6 15.♘e5 ♘a4 16.♖c2 ♘xb2+ 17.♖xb2 c3, and White was in deep trouble and soon lost.

9...♔e7 10.e3

Bluebaum-Giri went 10.a3 c3 11.axb4 cxb2 12.♖a2 ♖c8 13.♖xb2 ♖xc7

and Giri managed to exploit the misplacement of White's king.

10...♖c8 11.♗g3 ♗d5 12.♖c1 ♘bd7

13.♔e2! After 13...♘b6 White has 14.♗h4, and Black doesn't have time for ...♘a4, as White is threatening e3-e4, and with the king no longer on d1, Black can't take on b2 with check.

13...c3 14.bxc3 ♗xc3 15.♔d1 a5 16.♗d3 ♗xa2

And the drama petered out to a draw.

On the second day of the semifinal, after having won Game 3, Magnus just needed a draw in the fourth game to get to the final. What is the best strategy in such a case? To play calmly and solidly or to go for something ultra-sharp? Magnus chose the latter, or perhaps he was pushed to do so again by Aronian's aggressive play.

NOTES BY
Anish Giri

Magnus Carlsen
Levon Aronian
CCT New In Chess Classic 2021
(sf 2.4)
Sicilian Defence, Moscow Variation

1.e4 c5 Levon Aronian usually plays 1...e5, but it is hard to create winning chances there if White has his sights set on a draw – which would give Magnus Carlsen the so desired match victory.

2.♘f3 d6 3.♗b5+

A popular choice for must-not-lose situations in which White tries to weather the storm and avoids entering the popular Najdorf, in hopes of getting a slower, more positional game.

3...♘c6 4.0-0 ♗d7 5.♖e1 e5?!

In a must-win situation, Levon decided to improvise and create a mess from the very start. The main move here is the usual 5...♘f6.

6.c3 g5?!

A spirited idea, dictated by the match situation, but here it is really not a great moment for this theme.

7.d4! White strikes in the centre, as a response to Black's kingside adventure.

7...g4 8.♘fd2 exd4 9.♘a3!?

Clever and strong. Also good was the prosaic 9.♗xc6 ♗xc6 10.cxd4.

9...♕f6?! It is hard to double down on Black's overambitious opening, but Levon tries to stay true to the uncompromising spirit of his play.

10.cxd4 cxd4

11.e5!?

This works very well, essentially forcing matters.

11.♘ac4 0-0-0 12.♗xc6 ♗xc6 13.♘b3 leads to a winning position for White. Black has the bishop pair and an advanced g-pawn, but is too far behind in development, and the g-pawn can't do much damage to White's safe king on its own.

11...dxe5 12.♘ac4

Continuing the sequence. White will eventually regain both pawns.

12...0-0-0 13.♗xc6 ♗xc6 14.♘xe5

14...♗d5?

It is a bit late to advise Black, but perhaps 14...♘e7 would have offered more resistance. With the text-move Black completely ignores the development of his kingside, trying to hang on to his only trump, the light-squared bishop.

15.♕xg4+ ♕e6

Black has nothing better than this. The endgame is lost, and risk-free for White, which really helps.

16.♕xe6+ ♗xe6 17.♘df3

White starts untangling his pieces, getting his forces ready to pick up the weak d4-pawn.

17...♗b4 18.♖d1 ♖d5 19.♗f4

Magnus is ruthless in the rest of the game. The d4-pawn will fall anyway, and now ♖ac1 is coming as well.

19...♗c5 20.♖ac1 ♔d8

21.♘xf7+! The finishing blow. The rest is easy. **21...♗xf7 22.♗e5**

♘e7 22...♖xe5 23.♘xe5 ♗h5 24.g4 is no solution either. **23.♗xh8 ♘c6**

24.♖xc5!? Torture. The endgame is hopeless for Black. **24...♖xc5 25.♘xd4 ♔c7 26.♘xc6 ♔xc6 27.a3**

With two pawns up and connected passed pawns, White is completely winning. Levon still tried to salvage the game, but it was a hopeless mission.

27...♖d5 28.♖xd5 ♔xd5 29.f3 ♔c4

CCT New In Chess 2021 (prelims)

			elo rapid		TPR
1	Carlsen	NOR	2881	10½	2852
2	Nakamura	USA	2829	9½	2801
3	Mamedyarov	AZE	2761	9½	2806
4	So	USA	2741	9	2784
5	Aronian	ARM	2778	9	2782
6	Firouzja	FID	2703	8½	2758
7	Le Quang Liem	VIE	2744	8½	2755
8	Radjabov	AZE	2758	8½	2754
9	Dominguez	USA	2786	8	2730
10	Tari	NOR	2531	7	2711
11	Vidit	IND	2636	7	2704
12	Praggnanandhaa	IND	---	7	2700
13	Duda	POL	2774	7	2695
14	Karjakin	RUS	2709	6½	2717
15	Jones	ENG	2615	3	2487
16	Christiansen	NOR	2521	1½	2372

30.♔f2 ♔d3 31.♗c3 b5 32.g4 a6 33.♔g3 ♔e3 34.f4 ♔e4 35.f5 h5 36.h3 hxg4 37.hxg4

Black resigned. The connected pawns will cost Black the bishop, as White's king marches through h4 and g5.

■ ■ ■

Rapid gladiators

Now everything was set for another clash between perhaps the biggest rapid gladiators of our time. Magnus and Nakamura have met as many as 203 times, with mostly decisive outcomes. The score is overwhelmingly in Magnus's favour, but Nakamura has beaten him 32 times, more than anyone else in the world. After two draws Magnus was about to outplay his opponent in Game 3, but, surprisingly, he blundered a piece.

Magnus Carlsen
Hikaru Nakamura
CCT New In Chess Classic 2021
(final 1.3)

position after 25...♖d7

26.♖ad1 Magnus explained that he'd seen 26.♗xb7 ♖xb7 27.e5 ♕e7 28.exd6 ♕d7 29.♖e7, winning, but perhaps his sense of harmony had made him want to include the rook on the open file first.

26...♖e8 27.♗xb7? Too late!
27...♖xb7 28.e5 ♕e7 29.exd6 ♕d7 30.♖xe8+ ♕xe8

The rook is taboo due to 31...♗e4+. Luckily for Magnus, he got three pawns for the piece and the position was balanced. Many moves later Nakamura blundered:

To his shock Hikaru Nakamura realizes that his error 46...♕f8? has left Magnus Carlsen with a winning queen ending.

46...♕f8?? 47.♕f5+ ♔c6 48.♕c5+ ♔d7 49.♕f5+ ♔c6 50.♖xd6+! ♕xd6 50...♔xd6 51.♕c5+ skewers the king and queen. **51.♕xf7 ♕d2+ 52.♔g3 ♕xc3**

and Magnus won the queen ending in exemplary fashion. It was just a matter of putting the queen in the middle, protecting all the pawns and heading forward with the king.

Magnus also won the fourth game on the first day, and it looked like turning into a walk in the park for him. However, the next day started with Nakamura winning, and suddenly it was all open again.

Hikaru Nakamura
Magnus Carlsen
CCT New In Chess Classic 2021 (fin 2.1)
Nimzo-Indian Defence, Classical Variation

1.d4 ♘f6 2.c4 e6 3.♘c3 ♗b4 4.♕c2 d5 5.cxd5 exd5 6.♗g5 h6 7.♗h4 c5 8.dxc5 ♗e6 9.e3 0-0 10.♘f3 ♘bd7 11.♘d4 ♗xc5 12.♗d3 ♗xd4 13.exd4 ♕b6 14.♕d2

14...♘e4!? Typically, Magnus goes for the most active approach.
15.♗xe4 15.♘xe4 dxe4 16.♗xe4 f5 spells all kinds of trouble for White.
15...dxe4 16.d5 ♗f5 17.0-0 ♕g6 18.d6

CCT New In Chess 2021 (KO finals)

Quarter Finals

Carlsen-Radjabov	2-2	2½-1½
Aronian-So	3-1	2-1
Mamedyarov-Firouzja	3-1	2½-½
Le Quang Liem-Nakamura	1½-2½	1-2

Semi-Finals

Carlsen-Aronian	2-2	3-1	
Mamedyarov-Nakamura	1-3	3-0	1-2

Final 3rd-4th place

Aronian-Mamedyarov	2-2	½-2½

Final

Carlsen-Nakamura	3-1	2-2

Magnus seems to have misjudged the position. Nakamura has a wonderful passed pawn, and soon the pieces will come and back it up.

18...♞e5 19.♗g3 ♖fe8 20.♞b5
There are lots of tempting ideas for White here.

20...♖ad8 21.♕c3 ♞c6 22.♞c7 ♖f8 23.♖ad1 h5 24.♞c5
24.h4 or 24.h3 was also possible.

24...♖d7

25.b4 25.♖d5! was extremely tempting, but Nakamura's idea is also OK.

25...a6 26.a4 e3
It doesn't quite work, but at least Black gets some activity.

27.fxe3 ♗e4

28.♖d2

28.♞d5! was even more effective.

28...♚h7
Actually Magnus had a chance here to get rid of the horrible d-pawn with 28...h4 29.♗xh4 b6!, but the outcome should still be the same.

29.b5 axb5 30.axb5 ♞d8 31.♞d5 ♞e6 32.♕c4 h4 33.♞e7 ♕g4 34.♗e5 ♞g5 35.♗f4??
Nakamura has been completely winning all along, but now the computer arrow pivoted completely.

35...♞h3+?
A few moves later we suddenly saw Magnus very upset. It was probably the moment he discovered he could have won the game with the brilliant 35...♖xd6!. 36.♗xd6+ loses to 36...♞h3+ 37.♚h1 ♗xg2+, and the queen falls, and without the d-pawn, White has nothing.

36.♚h1 f5 37.♕e6 ♞xf4 38.♖xf4 ♖a8

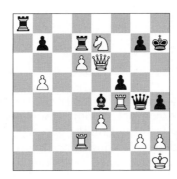

39.♚g1
Nakamura just has to handle some more tricks, but 39.♕e5 was much simpler.

39...♖a1+ 40.♖f1 ♖xf1+ 41.♚xf1 ♖d8 42.h3 ♕g5

43.d7! Nakamura calculated this to the end. 43...♕xe3 44.♕g6+ ♚h8 45.♕h5+ ♕h6 46.♕e8+ ♚h7 47.♕xd8

47...♗xg2+ The last desperate attempt. **48.♚e2 ♗f1+ 49.♚d1 1-0.**

Nakamura seemed to have a wonderful position in Game 2, too, but for some reason he accepted a draw by repetition. Perhaps he had planned to draw the remaining two games, and wanted to save energy for the tiebreak. A very strange thing then happened in Game 3. Tactical blunders are frequent, even at this level, but the key moment in this game seems more like a giant positional blunder.

Tactical blunders are frequent, even at this level, but the key moment in this game seems more like a giant positional blunder

NOTES BY
Peter Heine Nielsen

Hikaru Nakamura
Magnus Carlsen
CCT New In Chess Classic 2021
(final 2.3)
Queen's Gambit Declined, Janowski Variation

1.d4 d5 2.c4 e6 3.♘c3 a6!?

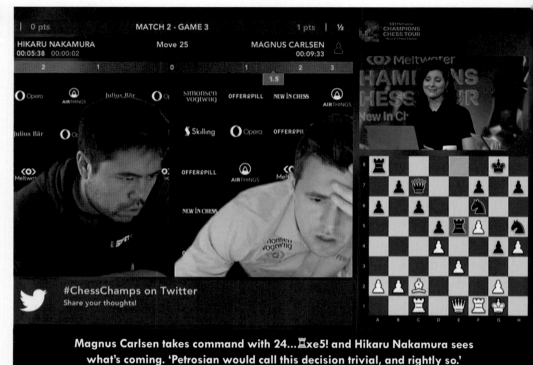

Magnus Carlsen takes command with 24...♖xe5! and Hikaru Nakamura sees what's coming. 'Petrosian would call this decision trivial, and rightly so.'

Having won Day 1, Magnus only needed a 2-2 result to clinch the title. However, Day 2 had started badly, when he lost with the black pieces. After Game 2 had ended in a draw, Magnus had to win one of the next two games to avoid a playoff. He decided to avoid a theoretical battle and go for this pet line, which tends to lead to very playable – though slightly worse – positions. The move might look odd, but the threat of ...dxc4, after preparing ...b5, forces White to release the tension in the centre.

4.cxd5 exd5 5.♗f4 ♘f6 6.e3 ♗d6
7.♗xd6 Nakamura had previously opted for the more ambitious 7.♗g3, but in view of the match situation, he is obviously happy to simplify.
7...♕xd6 8.♗d3 ♗g4 9.♕b3 ♘c6 10.h3 ♗h5

11.♘ge2 Taking the pawn – 11.♕xb7 – is an option, but after 11...0-0 12.♕b3 ♖ab8 Black does get some initiative for the pawn. So Nakamura once again keeps it simple.
11...♗xe2!? An interesting decision. The bishop, generally speaking, is rated somewhat higher than the knight by modern standards, but since one set of bishops has already been exchanged, White will be unable to secure the bishop pair. Because this also slightly unbalances the position, it gives Magnus some scope for outplaying his opponent, even though White nominally is a tad better.
12.♘xe2 0-0

13.♖c1
13.g4!? was the ambitious way here, but Nakamura had already clearly indicated that this was in no way his intention in this game.
13...♘d8 14.♕a3

14...♕d7!
Exchanging the queens on a3 would leave White with isolated doubled pawns, of course, but this doesn't seem to be of much consequence in this set-up. After the queen swap White could easily follow up with f3, g4, etc., keeping the position both safe and slightly better.

15.0-0 g6 16.♘f4 ♖e8 17.♗c2 c6 18.♘d3 ♘e6

19.f4

Nakamura has been making standard moves and is finding it hard to improve his position further. He could, and should, have started treading water, but that would have allowed Magnus to reinforce his set-up with moves like ...♖e7, ...♖ae8, ...h5, ...♔g7, etc. So there is logic in his play, although it backfires horribly.

19...♘g7 20.f5 g5!

Champions Chess Tour standings		
		TPR
1 Carlsen	185	$95,000
2 Wesley So	145	$85,000
3 Radjabov	109	$78,500
4 Giri	105	$75,000
5 Nepomniachtchi	83	$60,000
6 Aronian	81	$66,500
7 Nakamura	73	$45,000
8 Vachier-Lagrave	54	$46,500
9 Dubov	23	$25,000
10 Mamedyarov	21	$13,500
11 Firouzja	9	$12,500
12 Duda	3	$10,000
13 Le Quang Liem	2	$2,500

Suddenly White has irreparably weakened his position. Black's knights are blocking the kingside, and the g5-pawn cannot easily be attacked. Nakamura had pinned his hopes on accessing the e5-square, but....

21.♘e5 ♕c7 22.h4 g4 23.♕c3 ♘gh5 24.♕e1

24...♖xe5!

Petrosian would call this decision trivial, and rightly so. In principle, it is a material sacrifice, but for the exchange Black gets a pawn and full control of the position, starting with the e-file and the e5-square. Later, we'll also see that giving Black access to the g3-square is what will really bring White down.

25.dxe5 ♕xe5 26.♕c3 ♕g3! 27.♕e1

27...♕d6

Not that all endgames wouldn't be better for Black, but with the white king potentially weak, keeping the queens on seems even more efficient.

28.♕f2 ♖e8 29.♖cd1 ♕e5 30.♖d4 c5 31.♖d2 ♘g3 32.♖fd1

32...♔f8 Not strictly necessary, but a sign of strength. Black can quietly reinforce his position even further, because White has absolutely no positive options.

33.♖d3 ♘fe4 34.♕e1

34...♕f6!

Attacking the h4-pawn. Once this pawn disappears, the white position collapses, as Black gets direct access to the king.

35.♖xd5 ♕xh4 36.♗xe4 ♕h1+ 37.♔f2 ♘xe4+ 38.♔e2 ♕xg2+ 39.♔d3

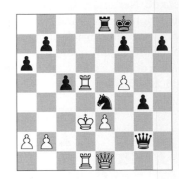

Now, with many moves winning, the simplest one may be 39...♘f2+, Nakamura resigned. With a draw in the fourth game Magnus clinched overall victory.

After an extremely wild match against Levon Aronian had brought him third place, Shakhriyar Mamedyarov told the studio in Oslo that rapid was his favourite time control.

The fight for third place between Aronian and Mamedyarov was extremely wild, with Black winning in six of the seven games and Mamedyarov ending up on top. I was particularly struck by another example of one of his specialties.

Levon Aronian
Shakhriyar Mamedyarov
CCT New In Chess Classic 2021
(final 3rd/4th 1.2)
Sicilian Defence, Four Knights Variation

1.e4 c5 2.♘f3 e6 3.d4 cxd4 4.♘xd4 ♘f6 5.♘c3 ♘c6 6.♘xc6 bxc6 7.e5 ♘d5 8.♘e4 ♕c7 9.f4 ♖b8!?

Mamedyarov beat both Nils Grandelius and Chithambaram Aravindh with this recently. The big question is how good the knight sacrifice 10.c4 ♗b4+ 11.♔e2 0-0 is.
10.a3 Both Grandelius and Aravindh played 10.♗d3.
10...♕b6 11.♕f3 ♗e7 12.c4 f5!

The typical counterstrike in these positions.

13.♘d2? Not this! **13...♘e3!** Mamedyarov gladly accepts the invitation. **14.♗d3 g5!** Black is backing up his outpost with great speed.
15.g3 gxf4 16.gxf4 ♖g8

This is basically it. Black already has plenty of resources to complete the attack.
17.♘f1 ♘g2+ 18.♔e2 ♕d4 19.♘g3 ♖xb2+ 20.♗xb2 ♕xb2+ 21.♔f1 ♘h4 0-1. ∎

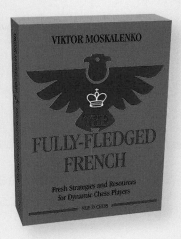

MAXIMize your Tactics

with Maxim Notkin

Find the best move in the positions below

Solutions on page 83

1. White to play

2. White to play

3. White to play

4. White to play

5. White to play

6. White to play

7. White to play

8. Black to play

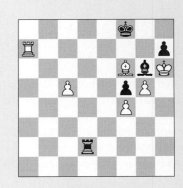

9. White to play

Women's GRAND PRIX

CALETA HOTEL May 22 - June 2, 2021

Gibraltar • The home of Women's Chess

www.gibchess.com   #gibchess

Judit Polgar

Garry Kasparov, a source of inspiration

First she was a fan, then a colleague and rival. These days they are friends and fellow promoters of the game. **JUDIT POLGAR** looks at the lessons she learned from Garry Kasparov. The opening and middlegame play of the 13th World Champion are rightly famous, but let's not forget about his endgame virtuosity either.

When, at the age of 12, I was taking part in the Olympiad for the first time – in Thessaloniki in 1988 – one of my main sources of inspiration was that I would be playing in the same hall as the reigning World Champion, Garry Kasparov. This feeling was especially strong when I noticed him watching my attacking win over Pavlina Chilingirova of Bulgaria with great interest.

However, Kasparov's games had started influencing my chess progress one year earlier, when my sister Sofia and I analysed in great detail the games of his fourth title match against Anatoly Karpov in Sevilla. We also wrote articles commenting on the match for a Hungarian newspaper. I still vividly remember the way he won the endgame of the dramatic 24th and final game.

Over the years, I came to realize that Garry was the most emotional chess player I have ever known. His emotions may be intimately connected with his hyper-dynamic, uncompromising and straightforward playing style. He never made any effort to hide the fact that he was aiming to win every game as quickly as possible.

Trademark 1 – Master of the Sicilian

I cannot think of an opening that would describe Garry's style more accurately than the Najdorf and Scheveningen Sicilian. Over the years, he had been widening and adjusting his Black repertoire against 1.d4 and his White repertoire generally, but for a very long time he only used the aforementioned Sicilian systems against 1.e4.

My first over-the-board encounter with Garry offered me an insight into his subtle understanding of the Sicilian. I recommend for you to

follow the trajectory of his pieces, especially the rooks and the knights.

Judit Polgar
Garry Kasparov
Linares 1994

position after 12.♔h1

Black has played a provocative line, based on quick queenside development at the cost of delaying kingside castling. This exposes him to the thematic threat e4-e5.

The game is complex enough to

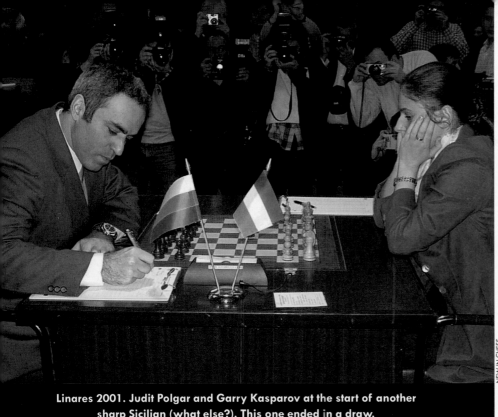

Linares 2001. Judit Polgar and Garry Kasparov at the start of another sharp Sicilian (what else?). This one ended in a draw.

correspond with more than just one trademark. Garry's opening approach can be described as **Trademark 2 – carrying out the main plan with maximum speed**. As mentioned above, this implies neglecting some other aspects, and requires perfect assessment and control of the situation.

12...♖d8!

A far from obvious move, since rooks are supposed to belong on open files. The main idea is to set up indirect pressure on the d4-knight to prevent the centre being opened.

12...0-0 would allow 13.e5 dxe5? (13...♘e8) 14.fxe5 ♘xe5 15.♗xb7 ♘eg4 16.♕g3, when the extra bishop is still alive on b7 and the knight on g4 is exposed to h2-h3.

13...♘e8 is better, but offers Black fewer perspectives for counterplay than the game move.

13.♗e3

With the rook on d8, 13.e5? won't

work: 13...dxe5 14.fxe5 ♘xe5 15.♗xb7 (the pin created by 15.♗f4 is ineffective due to 15...♘xf3!, winning) 15...♖xd4 (the point) 16.♗xa6 (the threat ♘b5 looks unpleasant, but Black can launch his counterplay in time) 16...♘eg4 17.♗b5+ ♔f8, with a decisive attack against the poorly defended white king.

13...0-0

14.♕g3

Black has completed his development harmoniously, but things are not

stable in the centre yet. If allowed to prepare e4-e5 with ♖ae1, my position would be very promising.

14...♘c5!

The first move out of the basic set-up, aiming at stabilizing the centre.

15.f5

Forced, since 15.e5 dxe5 16.fxe5 ♘fe4 is excellent for Black.

15...e5 16.♗h6 ♘e8

The second knight abandons its optimal square.

17.♘b3

17...♘d7!

The knight has done its job on c5 and returns to its main square. Black needs to keep the c-file open and the white pawn on c2 as a target.

It is interesting to notice that the central structure is blocked, and in the next phase we will both move only our pieces.

18.♖ad1 ♔h8 19.♗e3 ♘ef6?!

Kasparov continues the process of improving his coordination, but this move prematurely exposes the knight to the advance of my g-pawn. As pointed out by himself, now was a good moment to start the queenside counterplay: 19...b5! 20.axb5 axb5

Garry never made any effort to hide the fact that he was aiming to win every game as quickly as possible

21.♕f2 b4 22.♘d5 ♗xd5 23.♖xd5 ♘ef6!. This is a good moment for the knight's return. Black will continue with ...♖c8, with good counterplay.

20.♕f2

Suddenly, White's threat of g4-g5 is unpleasant.

20...♖fe8! Black starts improving the positions of his rooks, while at the same time preparing a central blow against my kingside.

21.♖fe1?! With this natural move, almost imitating Kasparov's, I did not only miss a good opportunity, but also slightly worsened my coordination, as is revealed below.

I should have had the courage to play 21.g4! d5! 22.♘xd5! (it is best to get rid of this knight before it becomes a target: 22.exd5 e4 23.♗e2 ♗a3! 24.d6!? ♗xd6 25.g5 ♘g8, with unclear play) 22...♘xd5 23.exd5 e4.

ANALYSIS DIAGRAM

It is obvious now that the rook stands well on e8, even though its action is latent. In the event of 24.♗xe4 ♘f6

25.♗f3 ♗xd5, Black has fantastic play for the pawn, but after the calm 24.♗g2 his compensation is not so obvious.

21...♗f8 Adding further force to the central break.

22.♗g5 With the rook on e1, 22.g4 d5 works well for Black: 23.♘xd5 ♘xd5 24.exd5 e4 25.♗g2 ♘f6. The double threats on d5 and g4 shatter the stable position of my bishop on e3. The point is that after 26.♗xb6? ♘xg4! my queen would no longer be defended by the rook.

22...h6 23.♗h4 ♖c8! The rook finally reaches its natural square. Black's coordination seems perfect, but Kasparov continues his manoeuvring.

24.♕f1 ♗e7 The bishop, too, returns to its previous location, preparing certain tricks based on a discovered attack, ...♘xe4, for instance.

25.♘d2 ♕c5 26.♘b3 ♕b4

Neither of us has moved a single pawn since 15...e5. Using 'imperceptible' moves, Garry has reached a slightly more pleasant position, but not an advantage yet.

27.♗e2? Cracking under the pressure. **27...♗xe4!** Due to the vulnerability of my c2-pawn, I had no favourable way to take on a6. Black had an overwhelming advantage at this stage and Garry eventually won after some mutual time-trouble adventures (0-1, 46).

At a superficial glance, little seems to have happened in the static phase of this game. However, I find Garry's manoeuvres (especially those with the rooks) simply magical!

Trademark 3 – Persistence in the endgame

Regardless of Kasparov's wonderful opening preparation and middle-game play, his endgame technique and tendency to fight till the last resource have yielded him many wins, even in drawn endings. I have 'burnt myself' at least twice.

In Dos Hermanas 1996, I worked a few miracles in a lost position, reaching a drawn rook versus rook and knight endgame. Convinced that

I played carelessly and allowed Garry to reach a theoretical winning set-up, analysed by Luigi Centurini in the 19th century

the hardest part of the work had been done, I played carelessly and allowed Garry to reach a theoretical winning set-up, analysed by Luigi Centurini in the 19th century. Kasparov showed that he knew the theory well and won quickly.

In the next example, from a rapid game, I threw away the fruits of my long defence in just one move.

Judit Polgar
Garry Kasparov
Geneva 1996

position after 38...♖f5

I had been struggling for quite a while, but around here, I rightly felt that I should be able to reach a draw.

39.♖d4 ♗xf4 40.♖d8+ ♔c7 41.♖d7+ ♔c8 However, I relaxed prematurely at this moment and played:

42.♖xf7?

Prematurely freeing the black king. Before taking on f7, I should have weakened Black's kingside with 42.h4 ♗g3 43.h5 ♗f4 (43...gxh5 44.♖xf7 is even simpler) 44.hxg6 hxg6 45.♖xf7 (now is a good moment for taking) 45...♔d8 (the same trick as in the game fails to win after g6 has become weak) 46.♖xf5 gxf5 47.♗f7 ♔e7 48.g6, with a draw. Because of my passed pawns, Black will not unable to coordinate his forces in order to advance his connected pawns.

42...♔d8!

With my pieces hanging, I needed to release the tension now, helping Black to improve his structure. Even worse than that, I will lose both my kingside pawns soon.

43.♖xf5 exf5 44.♗f7 ♔e7 45.♗g8 ♔f8! Shattering my last hopes.

46.♗d5 46.♗xh7 ♔g7 traps the bishop. **46...♗xh2 47.♔c2 ♗f4** and Kasparov won (0-1, 60).

Conclusions

■ You should aim at having at least one opening that you know inside out.

■ Maximizing the speed of the execution of the main plan puts pressure on your opponent, but requires accurate handling.

■ One should never forget that the apparent simplicity of an endgame may hide many subtleties. ■

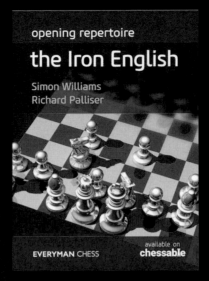
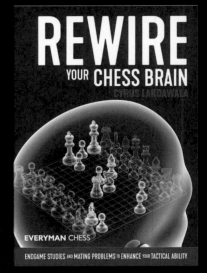
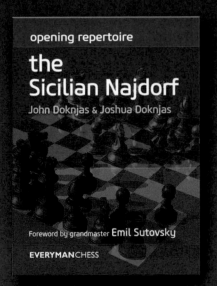
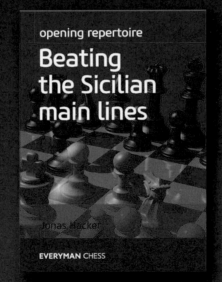
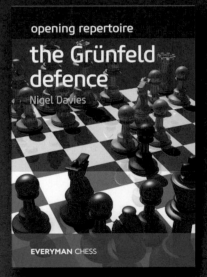

Thomas Willemze

What would you play?

One of the earliest lessons we learn is to safely tuck away our king so it will come to no harm. But it should not be forgotten that the king can also be an active piece, bravely taking part in an attacking game.

Bringing your king to safety is one of the golden rules in chess. The safest spot is usually the corner, but in some cases it is also possible to leave your king in the middle, where it can either find shelter behind a closed pawn centre, or rely on a well-organized army for its protection.

Exercises

Stefan Pricopie (1630) took the concept of a centralized king to a whole new level at the U-16 World Youth Championship in Maribor, Slovenia, in 2012. In his game against Henning Jakhelln Kjoita (1992) from Norway, the young Romanian literally put his king in the centre and won an amazing game. I selected four exercises that teach us the benefits (and dangers!) of the centralized king.

Exercise 1

position after 9...♘h5

White has started the game aggressively, and now has several attractive

moves available. He can trap a knight on the rim with 10.g4, attack a pinned knight with 10.e6, or stabilize his centre with 10.♘f3. **What would you play?**

Exercise 2

position after 13...♘xg3

White clearly lost control during the last four moves and needs to be quite precise to keep an equal game. **What would you recommend?** Should White attack the queen with 14.♘f3, pin the knight with 14.♕e1 or play 14.hxg3 and sacrifice an exchange?

Exercise 3

position after 18.♔d3

This position did not occur in the game, but it serves as a warning. Centralizing your king is never without risk! Black has two different mate-in-two moves available. **Can you find them?**

Exercise 4

position after 18...♕g2

The white king is on a roll! Should he take the next step with 19.♔xd6, or is it safer to trade pieces with either 19.♗xd7 or 19.♕e2 to neutralize the annoying black queen?

I hope you enjoyed these exercises and feel inspired by this brave centralized king. You can find the full analysis of this game on the next pages.

White takes the concept to a whole new level as he literally puts his king in the centre and wins an amazing game

Stefan Pricopie (1630)
Henning Kjoita (1992)
Maribor Wch U-16 2012
Benoni Defence, Four Pawns Attack

1.d4 ♘f6 2.c4 c5 3.d5 e6 4.♘c3 exd5 5.cxd5 d6 6.e4 g6 7.f4 ♗g7 8.♗b5+

The aim of this check is to disturb Black's coordination by forcing him to put a piece on d7.

8...♘bd7

This move rolls out the red carpet for the e4-pawn and has a dubious reputation. The counter-intuitive 8...♘fd7 deprives White of the option to push his centre pawn with tempo and is, therefore, the main move.

9.e5! ♘h5

10.e6!

This was the right solution to **Exercise 1**. White can only secure a clear advantage if he marches on with his e-pawn. 10.♘f3 gives Black just enough time to safeguard his king with 10...dxe5 11.fxe5 0-0, while 10.g4 leads to a complex position after 10...♕h4+ 11.♔f1 ♘g3+ 12.hxg3 ♕xh1.

We should thank White for this brave move, as it will be the impetus for a highly entertaining game

10...♕h4+ 11.♔d2

We should thank White for this brave move, as it will be the impetus for a highly entertaining game.

The boring truth, however, is that 11.♔f1! would have been much stronger. White has a relatively safe king and will soon be able to collect the black knight and acquire a winning advantage. He must realize that there is no need to fear 11...♘g3+ 12.hxg3 ♕xh1.

ANALYSIS DIAGRAM

This position arose in four different games. In two of them, Black resigned immediately after 13.♕a4, even though 13.♕g4! is even stronger. This move enables White to trade queens with ♕h3 after collecting the loot at d7.

11...fxe6

12.g3 White spoils valuable time and hands over the initiative to his opponent. The simple 12.dxe6! was the right way to go. White will be able to develop a large initiative after 12...♗xc3+ 13.bxc3

ANALYSIS DIAGRAM

13...♕xf4+ 14.♔c2 ♕e4+ 15.♔b2 ♕xe6 16.♘f3.

12...♗xc3+

It was unnecessary to give up this bishop. 12...♘xg3 13.♕e1 a6! would have been stronger, even though I must admit that the ensuing complications are very difficult to assess in a practical game.

ANALYSIS DIAGRAM

14.dxe6 axb5 15.exd7++ ♔xd7 16.♕xg3 ♕xg3 17.hxg3

ANALYSIS DIAGRAM

It is a pity that we can only enjoy the symmetry in this position for a very brief moment, since the black king will find a very comfortable spot with 17...♔c6. Black's powerful bishops and superior king promise him more than enough compensation for the piece.
13.bxc3 ♘xg3

14.♘f3
The key to **Exercise 2** was to coordinate a well-organized army around the exposed white king. We will soon discover that the game continuation fails to achieve this goal.
14.hxg3 won't work either, since Black can simply collect the exchange and

centralize his queen with 14...♕xh1 15.dxe6 ♕d5+! 16.♔c2 ♕xe6.
The right solution, therefore, was 14.♖e1!. White is about to use the black queen as a target to coordinate his pieces with tempo: 14...♕xf4+ 15.♔c2 ♕f5+ 16.♗d3 ♕xd5 17.hxg3 ♕xh1 18.♕xe6+ ♔d8 19.♗f4.

ANALYSIS DIAGRAM

White is an exchange and two pawns down, but will have decent compensation this time due to his well-coordinated forces.
14...♘e4+ 15.♔e3

15...♕f2+
This is a very logical move, which drives the white king towards the

centre. However, 15...♕f6! would have been much stronger, because it would have enabled Black to finally get rid of the annoying pin and coordinate his forces after 16.♔xe4 a6!. The annoying bishop on b5 was seriously hampering the development of Black's pieces. 17.♗xd7+ ♗xd7 18.dxe6 ♕xe6+ 19.♔d3 ♗b5+!.

ANALYSIS DIAGRAM

Black does not have many pieces left, but they are well-coordinated and extremely dangerous. White is in serious trouble after 20.♔d2 0-0.
16.♔xe4

16...♔d8

This is too slow and hands over the initiative to White. The straightforward 16...exd5+! 17.♔xd5 0-0 looks very dangerous for White.

17.♖f1! Well played! Taking the pawn, 17.dxe6, looks tempting, but gives Black the time to activate his pieces with 17...♘f6+! 18.♔d3 ♗xe6.

17...exd5+

18.♔xd5! White did, again, find the most accurate move. There was no way back, since here 18.♔d3 would have led to **Exercise 3**.

COLOPHON

PUBLISHER: Allard Hoogland
EDITOR-IN-CHIEF:
Dirk Jan ten Geuzendam
HONORARY EDITOR: Jan Timman
CONTRIBUTING EDITOR: Anish Giri
EDITORS: Peter Boel, René Olthof
PRODUCTION: Joop de Groot
TRANSLATOR: Piet Verhagen
SALES AND ADVERTISING: Remmelt Otten

PHOTOS AND ILLUSTRATIONS IN THIS ISSUE:
Maria Emelianova, Eteri Kublashvili, Hartmut
Metz, Lennart Ootes, V. Saravanan,
David Shifren, Berend Vonk

COVER ILLUSTRATION: Paul Kusters

COVER DESIGN: Hélène Bergmans

© No part of this magazine may be reproduced,
stored in a retrieval system or transmitted in any
form or by any means, recording or otherwise,
without the prior permission of the publisher.

NEW IN CHESS
P.O. BOX 1093
1810 KB ALKMAAR
THE NETHERLANDS

PHONE: 00-31-(0)72-51 27 137
SUBSCRIPTIONS: nic@newinchess.com
EDITORS: editors@newinchess.com
ADVERTISING: otten@newinchess.com

WWW.NEWINCHESS.COM

ANALYSIS DIAGRAM

The two correct mates in two were 18...♘e5+ 19.fxe5 ♗f5 and 18...c4+ 19.♗xc4 ♘c5.

18...♕g2

19.♔xd6! Kudos for White's brave (and strong!) move. This was the correct solution to **Exercise 4**. He rightly assessed that he has to keep his pieces on the board, since it will be Black's king that finds itself exposed.

19...♖e8

This is the decisive mistake in the game. Black's best bet would have been to push back the unleashed white king with 19...♖f8! and 20...♖f6+, even though White will still be clearly on top.

20.f5! White adds another powerful bishop to the attack.

20...♖f8 21.♗g5+ ♔e8 22.♕d5 ♖f7

This could have been an Exercise as well. Can you find another mate-in-two move?

23.♖ae1+ This is not the correct solution, but it leads to the same result.
23.♕e5+ ♔f8 24.♕h8 mate would have been the shortest route to victory.

23...♔f8 24.♗h6+ ♔g8 25.♖e8+ ♘f8 26.♖xf8

Mate. A beautiful picture, which encourages us to rethink our ideas about king safety!

Conclusion

White started the game hesitantly, but delivered a true masterpiece by fully exploiting his centralized king. This game does not change the golden rule that we should find a safe spot for our king in the opening, but has hopefully inspired you to unleash your creativity in your own games every once in a while. ■

MAXIMize your Tactics **Solutions**

1. Sjugirov-Naroditsky
Titled Arena 2021

34.♕xh7+! empties the d3-h7 diagonal: **34...♔xh7 35.♖h5+** Black resigned in view of 35...♖h6 36.♘g5++ ♔h8 37.♖xh6 mate.

2. Ipatov-Virtanen
chess.com 2021

The knight has to be given access to f6: **23.♖xd4! ♘xd4 24.♕xe8+!** Black resigned as after 24...♕xe8 25.♘f6+ he will be a piece down.

3. Shirov-Berzinsh
Gipslis Memorial lichess.org 2021

The famous pattern from Game 10 of the Petrosian-Spassky 1966 WCh Match: **21.♗xf7+ ♖xf7 22.♕h8+!** ♔xh8 23.♘xf7+ and White won.

4. Kraus-Sokolovsky
Israel ch Haifa 2021

The fastest way to win is **21.♕xf7+!** and Black resigned on account of 21...♖xf7 22.gxh7+ ♔h8 23.♘g6 mate. After first 21.gxh7+? ♔h8 22.♕xf7, 22...♘e5 turns the tables.

5. Nepomniachtchi-Pichot
Magnus Carlsen Invitational 2021

27.♘xe6! This discovered attack on the queen wins a piece for White after 27...♕xe4 28.♖xd8+ ♔b7 29.♘c5+ with a deadly fork. Therefore Black resigned.

6. Ippolito-Tarjan
lichess.org 2021

29.♘xe6! ♖xd3 The only reasonable reply. **30.♘xf8 ♖xd1+ 31.♔h2 h5 32.♕g5** and Black resigned since mate is imminent: 32...♔g8 33.♕h6.

7. Bodnaruk-Nasyrova
Moscow Open women 2021

White has enough resources to exploit a well-known motif twice: **21.♘hg6+! hxg6 22.♕h4+ ♔h7 23.♘xg6+ ♔g8 24.♘e7+ ♔h8** If 24...♔f7 25.♕h5+, mating on the next move. **25.♕xh7+!** There are no defenders left: 25...♔xh7 26.♖h5 mate. Black resigned.

8. Praggnanandhaa-A. Moskalenko
Titled Tuesday 2021

Black played 45...♖c1+ and even lost the game after blundering later on. The winning move was **45...h4!**. Allowing ...h4-h3 loses the e2-pawn, which is not an option for White. But in case of **46.♖h7 ♔f4! 47.♖xh4+ ♔g3 48.♖g4+ ♔h3** his king is caught in a mating net!

9. Dubov-Giri
Opera Euro Rapid 2021

White agreed to a draw by repetition: 51.♖a8+ ♔f7 52.♖a7+ ♔f8. No doubt he calculated **51.♖xh7!** ♗xh7 52.♔xh7 ♔f7 (52...♖c2 53.♗e5 and the passers decide) but didn't spot **53.♗g7!** which parries the mate threat and rolls out the red carpet for the g-pawn.

The Magnus Challenge

Always happy to inspire young talents, Magnus Carlsen took on 19 of the best juniors in a three-minute blitz marathon at the end of the Julius Baer Polgar Challenge. 'What a truly great guy do we have as our World Champion!' writes MAXIM DLUGY. And what great lessons can be learned from his games!

One spot in the New In Chess Classic was given to the winner of the Julius Baer Polgar Challenge, a rapid round-robin qualifier that brought together 20 of the world's top juniors, both male and female. The Polgar Challenge was a resounding success for Rameshbabu Praggnanandhaa, who earned the right to join 'the big boys'. The 15-year-old Indian swept the field, finishing one and a half points ahead of his closest rivals, Nodirbek Abdusattorov (Uzbekistan), Dommaraju Gukesh (India), Nihal Sarin (India) and Volodar Murzin (Russia), and two full points ahead of Germany's big hope Vincent Keymer.

Following the Polgar Challenge, Magnus Carlsen took on 19 of the juniors (sadly, Dinara Saduakassova had had to withdraw because of Internet issues), one after the other, in three-minute blitz games, giving the aspiring talents the chance to score their first win against a reigning World Champion – an amazing opportunity for these upcoming juniors.

Magnus' gesture reminded me of the great 'pioneer' exhibition matches in the Soviet Union, where the likes of Kasparov, Karpov, Kortchnoi, Spassky, Bronstein, Smyslov and Petrosian would take on the best Soviet youngsters. These master-classes jumpstarted the progress of these youngsters, creating the next generation of elite players in the Soviet Union. That the current World Champion is so magnanimous with his time to improve his upcoming competition is a clear sign of what a truly great guy we have as our World Champion! Thank you, Magnus!

True to his style and status, Magnus scored an impressive 16½ out of 19 against a field comprised of three 2600 players, six 2500 players and ten 2400 players. His only losses were against Awonder Liang (USA, 2592) and Nihal Sarin (2620), and he drew with Vincent Keymer (Germany, 2591).

In his game against Keymer, Magnus was also under serious pressure and had to defend a pawn down. Still there was an instructive moment, when he could have turned the tables if he had been faster than lightning.

Magnus Carlsen – Vincent Keymer
position after 52...⟨d7

At this point Magnus was down to six seconds, against 20 for Vincent, and the moves flashed by, as pre-moving

We should be grateful that the World Champion is so generous with his time to improve his upcoming competition

and avoiding a loss on time had become the only thing that mattered. Miraculously, the game ended in a draw by repetition.

Had Magnus had time to reflect in this position he would have found a nice win. Can you find it? The solution is given at the end of this article.

In the next game, against Carissa Yip, Magnus had time enough to spot a winning tactic.

Magnus Carlsen – Carissa Yip
position after 20...d5

Magnus didn't have to think long and struck almost instantly. Do you see how White can win quickly?
Solution of the puzzles on page 92.

The lessons that can be drawn from these blitz games are quite instructive, and I will try to explain some of the things young players should focus on when studying Magnus's games. For instance, in a number of games, Magnus decided to meet 1.d4 with the Benko Gambit, an excellent opening for blitz. Nursing an extra pawn to the finish line in a three-minute game forces White to spend extra seconds, which at some point become extremely valuable in a shorter time-control.

Dommaraju Gukesh
Magnus Carlsen
followchess.com
Carlsen vs Challengers 2021
Benko Gambit

1.d4 ♘f6 2.c4 c5 3.d5 b5 4.cxb5 a6 5.bxa6

This is the latest trend, although I still stand by the move 5.f3, which for some reason chess.com has dubbed the Dlugy Variation.
5...g6 6.♘f3 ♗g7 7.♘c3 0-0 8.g3 d6 9.♗g2 ♗f5

This move was introduced into GM practice by Veselin Topalov back in 1997. It is a valid alternative to recapturing on a6 with the bishop. Although only 40 games or so are found in the database, Black's results are quite good, and we can see that Magnus is quite well-versed in the theory of this opening as well.
10.♘d2 ♘xa6

11.e4?!
There is no reason to weaken the dark squares further, as White's d5-pawn cannot really be attacked. I think White needs to try and reason with Black's bishop positionally by manoeuvring his knight to e3. In that case, White can hope to retain a slight advantage. For example:
11.♘c4 ♘b4 12.♘e3 ♕c8 13.h3! ♗d7 14.a3 c4 15.♗d2 ♘a6 16.♖c1 ♖b8 17.♘a4 ♗xa4 18.♕xa4 ♘c5 19.♕xc4 ♖xb2 20.♘c3 ♖b3 21.♗b4, and White is a bit better.

Dommaraju Gukesh found out to his detriment that the Benko Gambit is a nasty weapon in blitz.

11...♗g4 12.f3 ♗c8!
The Moor has done his work, the Moor may go! White's weakened dark squares will now present excellent opportunities for Black.

Magnus vs Youngsters
time-control 3 min. no increment

Zhu Jiner (CHN)- **MC**	0-1
Praggnanandhaa (IND)-**MC**	0-1
MC-Zhansaya Abdumalik (KAZ)	1-0
Leon Luke Mendonca (IND)-**MC**	0-1
D. Gukesh (IND) — **MC**	0-1
Lei Tingjie (CHN)- **MC**	0-1
MC-Nihal Sarin (IND)	**0-1**
MC- R. Vaishali (IND)	1-0
S. Kademalsharieh (IRN)- **MC**	0-1
Yahli Sokolovsky (ISR)-**MC**	0-1
MC-P. Shuvalova (RUS)	1-0
MC-Jonas Buhl Bjerre (DEN)	1-0
Volodar Murzin (RUS)-**MC**	0-1
Olga Badelka (BEL)-**MC**	0-1
MC-Vincent Keymer (GER)	½-½
MC-Carissa Yip (USA)	1-0
Gunay Mammadzada (AZE)-**MC**	0-1
Christopher Yoo (USA)-**MC**	0-1
MC-Awonder Liang (USA)	**0-1**

13.a3 ♘b4

It's hard not to play this move in a three-minute game, but White's reply forces Black back. It was stronger to start prying the centre open with 13...e6! instead.

14.♘b3! ♘a6 15.0-0 ♘d7 16.♗e3 ♕b6 17.♖b1 ♘c7 Magnus is lining up his pieces to the best positions. White is hard-pressed to stop the invasion. **18.♘d2 ♗a6 19.♖f2 ♖fb8 20.♗f1 ♗xf1**

21.♔xf1? A nearly-decisive mistake, especially for blitz. White should have taken with the queen. After 21.♕xf1 ♕a6! 22.♕xa6 ♖xa6 23.♖ff1 ♖ab6 24.♘a4 ♖6b7 25.♖fc1 White could still hope to equalize. **21...♕a6+ 22.♕e2 ♗xc3 23.bxc3 ♕xa3**

Suddenly, White is simply lost. Black has regained the pawn and his pieces will invade the white position.

24.♖xb8+ ♖xb8 25.c4 ♘e5 26.♔g2 ♖b2 27.f4 ♘d3 28.♖f3 ♕c3 29.♔h3 ♕xc4 30.♕f1 ♕c2 31.e5 ♘xd5 32.f5 ♘xe5

White resigned. In this game we saw Gukesh not prepared in the opening.

Lesson 1: When preparing an opening system, you should look at less popular but statistically well-performing continuations (such as 9...♗f5) and have something ready to meet them.

One of the most common issues when players face Magnus is indecision based on fear!

One of the best prepared and highest-rated players on the junior circuit is Rameshbabu Praggnanandhaa. He not only won the Polgar Challenge by a wide margin, but he also had numerous chances to beat the World Champion in their blitz game. It's ironic that he lost only because his time ran out. Considering the age difference, 15 vs 30, one would think that his fingers should be getting those moves out faster than the World Champ's!

Rameshbabu Praggnanandhaa
Magnus Carlsen
followchess.com
Carlsen vs Challengers 2021
Queen's Pawn Game

1.d4 ♘f6 2.♗f4 Currently my favourite opening – so I am all ears. **2...e6 3.e3 b6 4.♕f3!?**

An excellent idea – especially for blitz. Magnus has to start thinking from the very first moves, while White has many interesting and complicated continuations to choose from – a dream sub-line for blitz!

4...♘c6 The 12 seconds Magnus took to reply indicate that he had not analysed this move deeply, and was choosing between this and the equally logical 4...d5.

5.♘c3 ♗b7 6.0-0-0 a6
Once again, a serious 16-second think from Magnus, who seemingly wants to stop a possible ♘b5, followed by c4, as well as start his counterattack with ...b5. Previously, Pragga had played against 6...♗b4 twice in this position, so Magnus's move prompts him to take a little time on his reply.

7.e4 This forces Black to consider his defensive plan. 7.d5 and 7.h4 are quite interesting as well.

7...b5 Played briskly by Magnus and quite provocative. Probably best was 7...d5!?, the point being that 8.exd5 is met by 8...♘e7!, with a great position.
8.d5 ♘e7

9.a3?! And here we come to one of the most common issues when players face Magnus – indecision based on fear! When analysing such games, I have found that, very often, when it was time to act aggressively, most players continued to prepare their ideas instead of actually executing them. Here as well, White should have lunged out with 9.g4!, forcing Black on the defensive. Black should now play 9...♘g6 (9...b4 10.g5 bxc3 11.gxf6 cxb2+ 12.♔b1 gxf6 13.♗c4 is dreadful for Black, with his king stuck in the middle) 10.♗g3 h5! 11.g5 ♘g4 12.h4 ♗d6! 13.♗h3 ♘4e5 14.♕g2, with an unclear position which offers White excellent attacking chances.
9...♘g6 10.♗g3 b4 I prefer 10...e5!, with a very nice position, when Black simply gets to attack on the queenside for free. But it looks as if Magnus sensed fear and decided to play on that, forcing White to start thinking to catch up with him on the clock.
11.axb4 ♗xb4

12.♗c4?! Once again Pragga refuses to attack, showing more indecision. After 12.h4! h5 13.dxe6 fxe6 14.♕d3 White has an edge.
12...0-0 It's strange that Magnus spent a whopping 39 seconds on this move. And also interesting that he refuses to play ...e5 and lock up the centre.
13.♘ge2 ♕e7 14.h4! h5 15.e5

15...♘g4? Played instantly, but taking on d5 was actually far stronger.
16.d6! It seems that Magnus simply missed this move, as he spent 37 seconds on his reply.
16...cxd6

17.♕xb7?
One second, really? If a World Champion doesn't like his position, there is probably a really good reason. Instead of the game continuation, Pragga could have considered 17.exd6 ♗xd6 18.♕xb7 ♗xg3 19.♖xd7 ♕f6 20.fxg3 ♘6e5 21.♗b3 ♖ab8 22.♕a7 ♘xd7 23.♕xd7, with a winning position. Spending time at the critical moments is crucial to good blitz play!
17...d5 18.♘xd5
The 27 seconds spent on this move indicate that White had missed

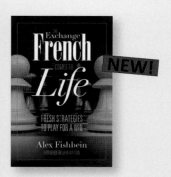

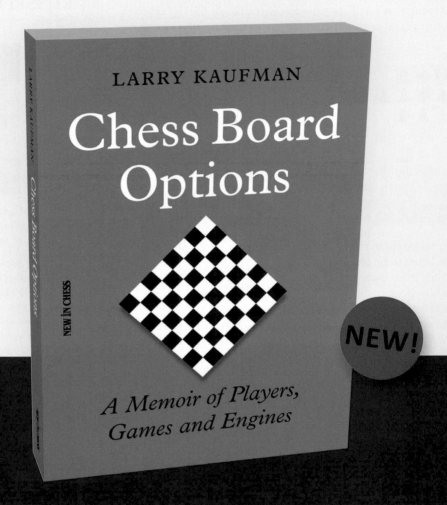

Black's reply. Though he is still much better, the time factor is now becoming the main element in evaluating the position, as White is down to 44 seconds, against Magnus with 43 seconds. Once the players enter bullet mode, each 10-second advantage is worth about a pawn in the position.

Though we should not judge the strength of the moves from now on – as both players were trying not to take more than a second per move – it is instructive how Magnus seeks to preserve time when playing in such circumstances, as he realizes that it is the clock that will most likely decide the outcome of the game.

18...exd5

19.♕xd5? A serious mistake. Taking with the rook would have kept a large advantage, which now dissipates. After 19.♖xd5! ♘4xe5? (19...♖fd8) 20.♖xe5 ♘xe5 21.♗xe5 White wins the bishop on b4.

19...♘6xe5 20.♗b3 a5 21.♗a4 ♖ac8 21...d6!, stabilizing the knights, would have been stronger.

22.♘d4 ♖c5

23.♕b3? White is trying to keep

Once the players enter bullet mode, each 10-second advantage is worth about a pawn in the position

Black from gaining a tempo with ...d5, but it was much more important to park the queen actively on the e-file. After 23.♕e4 d5 24.♕e2 White would be fine.

23...♕f6 Snuffing out the queen with 23...♘c4! would have given Black a serious advantage.

24.f3

24...♘h6? Black misses the intermediate move 24...♕h6+ 25.♔b1 ♘e3, with an advantage.

25.♔b1 ♘c4

26.♖d3? A strange blunder, as Black was clearly threatening a fork on d2. White could stop it with 26.♗e1.

26...♘d2+ 27.♖xd2 ♗xd2 28.♕d3 ♗f4 29.♗f2 ♖b8 30.♖d1 ♗e5 31.c3

And here Magnus blundered badly with:

31...♕b6?? Black had many moves to keep a decisive advantage, but 31...♖c7, removing the rook from the dangerous diagonal, made the most sense.

32.♘b3 d6

33.♗xc5
Played after one second, although enabling the capture on c5 with the knight by playing 33.♖d2! would have been nearly decisive. Once again, critical-time thinking is not working for Pragga.

33...dxc5 34.♕c4?
Giving away his advantage in one move. 34.♕e2! defends the g2-pawn and the b2-pawn, and attacks the bishop.

34...♕g6+ 35.♔a2?
The losing mistake! Though the move itself is fine – spending six seconds on it is suicidal. It doesn't matter what White plays at this point, as long as he does it quickly. Previous to this move White had 13 seconds left to Magnus's 19 – after this move the time difference can no longer be made up.

35...♕xg2 36.♕xc5 ♗f6

37.♕xh5?

This move blunders away the game, as Black can now win with 37...♗xc3, but both sides were in bullet mode now, trying not to spend more than a second per move.

37...♕c2?? 38.♖c1?

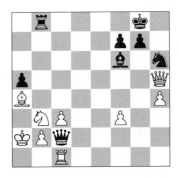

38...♕f5? The ending is no good for Black, but Magnus feels he can make moves faster in an endgame. After 38...♕d3 the position would have been roughly equal.

39.♕xf5 ♘xf5

40.♘c5?

White should simply have trusted himself and taken the pawn. There should be no additional modesty in playing the World Champion – as that is what gives him an extra edge!

40...♘d6 41.♘d7 After this move White was down to two seconds, so it really didn't matter anymore.

41...♖b7 42.♘xf6+ gxf6 43.♖g1+ ♔f8 44.♗c2 ♔e7 45.♗e4 f5 46.♗xb7 ♔f6 47.♖e1 ♘c4 48.♖d1 ♘xb2 49.♖d3 ♔e5 50.♖d4 ♘d3 51.f4+ ♔f6

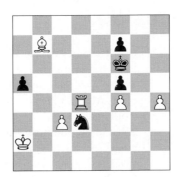

And white lost on time. Though the game was extremely hard fought, Magnus showed that when it comes to playing super-fast – he is the real king! He managed to outplay someone half his age easily, as he understands the true balance between position and time.

Lesson 2: To become a truly good blitz player it is crucial to cultivate this feeling of the inner clock, when you simply know when it is time to just play fast moves without hesitation.

Magnus showed that when it comes to playing super-fast – he is the real king!

Of course, sometimes Magnus just wins because of his superior positional understanding. In the following game, he breaks White down with one key stroke. Volodar Murzin, who is quickly becoming a serious player, goes down without a fight.

**Volodar Murzin
Magnus Carlsen**
followchess.com
Carlsen vs Challengers 2021
Zukertort Opening, King's Indian Attack

1.d3 d5 2.♘f3 ♘c6 3.g3 e5 4.♘bd2

4...♗e6

I am not sure I would play this move order against anyone, let alone the World Champion, as 4...f5 seems particularly strong, with the white knight on d2. The issue is that after 4...f5! 5.e4 dxe4 6.dxe4 fxe4 7.♘xe4 ♕xd1+ 8.♔xd1 ♗g4 9.♗e2 0-0-0+ 10.♘fd2 ♗f5 11.f3 ♘d4 Black simply has a better endgame.

5.♗g2 ♕d7 6.♘g5 ♗g4 7.h3 ♗h5

8.c3?

Once again, tentative chess. White should get into a full-fledged struggle with 8.c4 dxc4 9.♘xc4 f6 10.♘e4 ♘d4 11.g4 ♗f7 12.♗d2 0-0-0 13.♖c1, with a complicated game.

8...f6 9.♘gf3 ♗f7

Exploiting the bad knight on d2 with 9...f5! still seemed like the right idea.

10.b4 ♗d6

11.a4?!

This was White's chance to play in the centre. After 11.e4 d4 12.cxd4 ♘xb4 13.♘c4 White would stand well, as 13...♗xc4 14.dxc4 exd4 15.0-0 c5 16.e5! fxe5 17.♘xe5 ♗xe5 18.♕h5+ is too good for White.

11...♘ge7 12.e4?

What worked the previous move, no longer works here. One extra tempo plays a key role.

12...d4! 13.cxd4 ♘xb4

14.0-0

Now, after 14.♘c4 ♗xc4 15.dxc4 exd4 16.0-0 c5, 17.e5 no longer works, since Black has the ...♘g6 resource after ♕h5+.

14...exd4 15.e5 fxe5 16.♘e4 0-0

Magnus is up two pawns, and in the

Tentative play in the opening quickly got Volodar Murzin (14) in trouble.

remainder of the game the result was never in doubt (0-1, 33).

Lesson 3: Tentative play in the openings will almost always be punished severely by strong players (and certainly by the World Champion).

At the age of 20, Polina Shuvalova is already a very strong player. She is rated 2476 in the FIDE list, and in New In Chess 2021/2 you could read how close she came to winning the latest Russian Championship. Magnus plays extremely risky and aggressive chess against her, sacrificing unsoundly to see if she could refute his gambit play.

Magnus Carlsen
Polina Shuvalova
followchess.com
Carlsen vs Challengers 2021
Réti Opening, Neo-Catalan Declined

1.c4 e6 2.g3 d5 3.♗g2 ♘f6 4.♘f3 ♗e7 5.0-0 0-0 6.♕c2 b6 7.cxd5 ♘xd5 A somewhat strange decision, as White has an obvious edge, while 7...exd5 would have all the markings of a normal Queen's Indian/QGD setup for Black.

8.♘c3 ♗b7 9.♘xd5 ♗xd5

And once again Polina Shuvalova decides to keep the long diagonal

open, although 9...exd5 looks quite a bit safer.

10.e4 ♗b7 11.d4 c5 12.d5!?

Magnus thought for a whopping 32 seconds about this move, clearly believing his initiative would pay off. Stockfish evaluates this position as equal, so it makes it worthwhile in a three-minute game, as defending is always more time-consuming than attacking.

12...exd5 13.exd5 ♕xd5

Polina decided to accept the pawn, taking 28 seconds on this decision. It was also possible to play 13...♘a6, planning ...♘b4, with an equal game.

14.♘h4 ♕d7 15.♖d1

I am curious why Magnus took 19 seconds on this obvious move, which propels his attack. I simply don't see an alternative.

15...♕c8

Similarly, it is not clear what Polina was thinking about for 14 seconds. Since 15...♕c7 allows 16.♗f4, it's pretty clear that 15...♕c8 is forced.

16.♘f5 ♖e8 17.♗xb7

This was a tough choice and took 27 seconds off the champion's clock.

17.♕e2 was a very serious alternative, when Black's best would be 17...♘c6 18.♕g4 ♗f6 19.♗f4 ♔h8!, with a defensible position.

17...♕xb7

18.♗h6 This amazing shot was clearly prepared on the previous move, as it was pre-moved!

18...gxh6

Fully playable, but the much stronger defensive move 18...♗f8 would have given Black the advantage after 19.♗xg7 ♗xg7 20.♕c1 ♘c6 21.♘xg7. Now, to avoid the draw, Black would have to find 21...♖e5!! 22.♕h6 ♘d4 23.♖xd4 cxd4 24.♘h5 f6 25.♘xf6+ ♔h8, when Black is for choice.

19.♘xh6+ Objectively stronger was

19.♕e2, forcing 19...♔h8 20.♕e5+ f6 21.♕e6 ♘c6 22.♖d7 ♘d8!, when White can simplify into numerous endgames, but all of them equal.

19...♔h8!

20.♘xf7+?

Magnus spent 16 seconds on this move, but 20.♕f5! was stronger. Now, after 20...f6 21.♕g4 ♖f8 22.♘f5 ♖g8 23.♕e2 ♘c6 24.♕e6 ♘d4! 25.♕xe7 ♕xe7 26.♘xe7 ♖gd8, Black would be a tad better, as White would have to extricate the knight via the f5-square.

20...♔g7 21.♘d6 ♗xd6 22.♖xd6

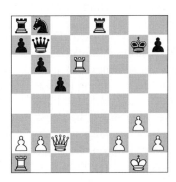

22...♘a6? In this position, evaluated as winning for Black by the engines, Polina had 27 seconds left, to Magnus's 17. It's pretty clear that

when one side has checks while the other has to defend, this advantage is just enough for Black to keep the balance. Still, after 22...♘d7! 23.♕c3+ ♔f8!! Black parries 24.♕h8+ with 24...♔e7 and a double attack! White has no attack left, as after 24.f4 ♖e2 25.♕h8+ ♔e7 26.♕xh7+ ♔xd6 27.♕d3+ ♔c7 28.♕xe2 ♕d5 29.♖d1 ♖e8! Black would be clearly winning.

23.♖ad1

23...♖e7?

The final mistake, but surviving was already near impossible, considering the time situation. Black had to play 23...♕e4 24.♕c3+ ♔g8 25.♖d7 ♖e5!, with an unclear but balanced game.

24.♕c3+ ♔g8 25.♕c4+ ♔g7 26.♕g4+ ♔f7 27.♕f5+

27...♔g8 28.♕g5+ ♔f7 29.♖f6+ ♔e8 30.♕g8 Mate.

Lesson 4: In a fast time-control players should seek to attack rather than defend. Having an attack adds value to your position, as your opponent will either spend extra time defending or will fail to see strong defensive moves and lose on the board. ∎

Solutions

Magnus Carlsen – Vincent Keymer
White could suddenly have knocked Black out with a left hook: 53.c4!!.
This forcibly wins material. E.g.: 53...♗xc4 54.♗a4+ ♗b5 55.♗xb5+ ♔xb5 56.♖xd7.

Magnus Carlsen – Carissa Yip
White starts attacking more than Black can defend: 21.♘g4! ♕d6 22.d4! dxe4 23.♘fxe5. This wins at least a piece, as Black cannot take care of f7, the knight on f4 and the queen on d6 with one reply. Carissa Yip went 23...♘fd5 24.♘xf7 ♕d7 25.♘xd8 ♖xd8 26.axb5, and then resigned.

They are The Champions

TUNISIA
Population: 12 million
Active rated players: 130

AMIR ZAIBI
Tunisia

GM Amir Zaib is the 2021 Tunisian champion. The championship was a 10-player round-robin tournament that took place in the Florya Crown Plaza hotel in... Istanbul, Turkey(!) between April 4th and 10th, 2021. The financial resources of the Tunisian chess federation are limited, and the new federation leadership and sponsorship took the championship abroad. The players were happy to visit a foreign country and play and stay in luxury accommodation. They all took a Covid PCR-test just before the tournament started, creating their own Covid-free bubble. The players would mask up whenever confronted with someone outside of their bubble.

With a rating of 2396, Amir Zaibi is the highest-rated player of Tunisia. He won the championship with a perfect 9 out of 9 score, reminiscent of Bobby Fischer's 11 out of 11 in the 1963/64 US Championship. Amir played like a judoka in the first few rounds, waiting to exploit his opponents' weaknesses created by his forcing moves. In the latter part of the tournament, he played more actively, often achieving his opponents' resignation before move 25.

Amir was awarded the grandmaster title after winning the 2019 Arab Championship in Algeria. Although he is happy to have obtained the title directly as a result of his victory in this event, he would like to have the opportunity to increase his insight in the game and take his rating from around 2400 to a (norm-based) grandmaster level. Amir is a full-time policeman and father of two and will need sponsorship to achieve that ambition.

In 2015 he was paired against Fabiano Caruana in the first round of the World Cup in Baku. Although there was no financial support from the Tunisian chess federation, he considered it a once-in-a-lifetime opportunity that he could not forego. After travelling for 28 hours, Amir went straight from the airport to the playing hall to play his game. He lost, but has never regretted the choices he made.

Amir is a versatile player who wins his games not only through positional means but also with tactical blows, as demonstrated in the following game.

Amir Zaibi (2249)
Zvonko Stanojoski (2434)
Mohamed Slama Memorial 2012
1.e4 c5 2.♘f3 g6 3.d4 cxd4 4.♕xd4 ♘f6 5.e5 ♘c6 6.♕a4 ♘d5 7.♕e4 ♘db4 8.♗b5 a6 9.♗a4 b5 10.♗b3 d5 11.exd6 ♗f5 12.♕e2 ♕xd6

In **They are The Champions** we pay tribute to national champions across the globe. For suggestions please write to editors@newinchess.com.

13.0-0 ♘a5 14.♖d1 ♕c7 Black's lack of development and unsafe king will prove fatal. White converts in spectacular fashion. **15.♗d2 ♘xb3 16.axb3 ♘xc2**

17.♕xb5+! ♗d7 The queen cannot be taken: 17...axb5 18.♖xa8+ ♗c8 19.♗a5 ♕xa5 (also hopeless is 19...♕d7 20.♖xd7 ♔xd7 21.♘e5+ ♔e6 22.♖xc8) 20.♖xc8, mate! **18.♖xa6! ♖b8** After 18...♗xb5 19.♖xa8+ ♕d8 20.♖xd8+ ♔xd8 21.♗c3+ Black can resign. **19.♕d5** White is winning and did not let his big fish off the hook. **19...e6 20.♕e4 ♘b4 21.♗f4 ♕c5 22.♗xb8 ♘xa6 23.♗e5 ♖g8 24.♘c3 ♕c6 25.♖a1 ♘c5 26.♖a8+ ♔e7 27.♕h4+ g5 28.♘xg5** 1-0.

Amir's best chess memory is the 2018 Chess Olympiad in Batumi. He felt invincible, and indeed remained undefeated, scoring 8½ out of 11 on Board 2 of Tunisia, including two draws against 2500+ grandmasters.

Amir dropped out of college, as he did not like to be bound by his professors' rules to solve scientific problems. This is also one of the reasons why he loves chess. Chess is Amir's universe, where he has the freedom to use his own logic and create his masterpieces. In this universe, there are only the FIDE Laws of Chess, the rest is left to his imagination. ■

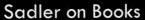

Repeating to improve

He is happy to spend hours analysing anything new, but why would he waste time going over stuff he already 'knows'? Because chess knowledge is trainable, as **MATTHEW SADLER** realized once again when he tried out a Chessable course. And he also read a couple of books that have just come out, of course.

A little while back, triggered by a Lawrence Trent tweet announcing his determination to finally secure the GM title once Covid restrictions were lifted, I got into a Twitter conversation about the challenges older players face to improve. I highlighted the difficulty in making space to focus on chess. By the time you reach your mid-30s, you've picked up many tasks and responsibilities – many of them positive, but still distracting – that you did not have in your teens and early twenties. Nigel Short bucked the trend of course by pointing out that his best results came in the years after his children were born – he explained to me once that the feeling of needing to provide for his children had motivated him enormously – but I think most people agreed with the sentiment.

Thinking about it some more, it struck me how much of the work I did as a young chess professional was simple repetition. (Re-)learning knowledge to ensure that it was repeatable on the one crucial occasion you needed it, whether it was my set of 200-300 endgames that I worked through at the start of every day or the continuous opening drills trying to perfect my recall of complicated variations. Funnily enough, 20 years later, I find this type of chess work excruciating. I'm happy to spend hours analysing anything new, but the prospect of sitting down and organising and learning what I've analysed (even once, let alone day after day!) is upsetting to the point of being distressing! Is it the feeling that my time left on this earth is now shorter than my time spent on it and that I'm not going to waste that time going over stuff I 'know' already?

Irrespective of the reason, repetition has benefits beyond simple memory. Repeating your analysis is a crucial part of clarifying your understanding of your chess personality. Taking out a board every day and playing out the variations you have chosen to fight with, reminds you – better than any other technique in my opinion – of the type of player you are and how you choose to tackle problems. That self-knowledge is an extremely valuable practical tool that proves invaluable in tense situations. Certainly, I feel that I have normally played my best – even recently – after a consistent period of playing through my openings, even if I rarely got any of that stuff on the board!

In the good old days as a chess professional, if I didn't like doing something, I'd merely tell myself to do it anyway. Nowadays, bearing in mind that chess is a hobby and supposed to be fun, I look for tools to help me. ChessBase has a Replay Training function but I haven't got it to work in a way that was useful to me. And then I thought of Chessable!

Chessable, for those of you who haven't tried it yet, is a website offering a mixture of books (such as *Game Changer*!) and Chessable-specific courses, with the emphasis on making chess knowledge trainable. Not only can you read through the course material with a digital chessboard displaying the moves – most courses have video content too – but you can also drill and repeat the moves to learn the material while you read it.

I hadn't looked at it for a long time, so I decided to try out one of the many Lifetime Repertoire courses on offer, which turned out to be *Sam Shankland's 1.d4* course, which is divided into three parts: Offbeat lines, 1...♘f6 (covering the Queen's Indian, King's Indian and the Grünfeld) and 1...d5 (covering the QGA, the QGD and the Semi-Slav). From the training perspective, each part is structured in the following way: after a brief introduction you dive into a Quick-Starter Guide which gives you a quick summary of the main lines covered. Having learnt those, you move on to chapters which deal with each of the openings covered in greater detail. Every step of the way, the variations analysed are unfolded for you step-by-step and you repeat them straight after (by default three times). Every successful repetition gets you points and there is an overall leaderboard to measure your progress against that of fellow learners. I've been doing a lot of Duolingo (gamified language learning) during the Covid lockdown (creating addicts of both my mum and her sister by recommending it to them!) and you recognise the same approach here of turning learning by repetition into a game. I was a little doubtful about doing this with chess to start with, but the approach does work very well. Perhaps the most important point is that the tool is responsive enough to allow you to pre-move your repetitions just like in a Lichess bullet game!

So, I like the tool, but how about the course? Shankland's stated goal is to present 'a repertoire based on the attitude I take to my own games whenever I open with the queen's pawn (...) the goal is not to tear Black's head off in the first 20 moves of the game, as one might see in some attacking repertoires. Rather, its goal is to fight for long-term advantages right from the first move of the game, including but not limited to extra space, a better structure, the bishop pair, etc...'

I completely agree with this approach. One of the big lessons I learnt as a young player was losing three crucial games as White in a Junior World Championship (including a heart-breaking last-round game). Despite being in good playing form, I couldn't cope game-in game-out with the tension of the hyper-sharp openings (Botvinnik Semi-Slav, Sämisch Nimzo-Indian, Knight Tour Benoni) that my newly-discovered love of opening analysis had brought to my repertoire!

Thinking 'what type of opening position would I have wanted to play in those crucial games?' was a key part in building a balanced repertoire that didn't burn my bridges from the first moment.

I also approve of Shankland building a lifetime repertoire around systems in which White plays ♘f3. One of my regrets as a 1.d4 player is that I standardised early on systems that expressly avoided ♘f3 (the Nimzo-Indian, Botvinnik systems with ♘ge2 against the Queen's Gambit Declined, the Sämisch King's

Repeating your analysis is a crucial part of clarifying your understanding of your chess personality

Indian). In the long term, it reduced the flexibility of my 1.d4 repertoire, not least by eliminating the possibility of using 1.♘f3 move orders to confuse Black! Shankland's choices are main line without being absolutely cutting-edge and there are some interesting twists, such as the Queen's Gambit Accepted where Tony Miles' 1.d4 d5 2.c4 dxc4 3.e3 ♘f6 4.♗xc4 e6 5.♘f3 c5 6.0-0 a6 7.♘bd2!?

gets a serious analysis. Tony scored 3½/4 with it in 1993 and 1994, using it as a clever way to get into 7.b3

Lifetime Repertoire
1.d4
Sam Shankland
Chessable, 2021
★★★★☆

systems while possibly confusing Black out of their intended system! Another cunning approach is 1.d4 d5 2.c4 e6 3.♘f3 ♘f6 4.♘c3 c6 5.e3 ♘bd7 6.♗e2

against the Semi-Slav which stays away from the reams of analysis on 6.♕c2 and 6.♗d3. Perhaps the only comment I might make about that was that I thought that 6.♗e2 ♗d6 7.0-0 0-0 8.b3 was quite well met by ...dxc4, either immediately or after a preliminary 8...♕e7 or 8...♖e8. For example, after 8...dxc4 9.bxc4 e5, Black follows up with ...♖e8, ...exd4 and ...♘f8-g6 with easy play. It's why I rejected these lines as White, but this plan does not seem to be covered by Shankland, as far as I can see.

Shankland's tone is sometimes a little forthright for my taste – 'The bishop on g7 is a moron' offended my sense of classical chess annotation practice – but there is no denying the quality and interest of the course! I haven't been through all of it yet – online courses take me much longer to get through than normal books! – but I'm enjoying it and I like what I've seen! 4 stars!

One final thing: while I was happily repeating moves and scoring points,

I was thinking how sad it was that I couldn't just upload my files to Chessable and drill my openings in my own personal course. Well... it seems that you can with the Create New Course option in the Tools menu. I'm not sure whether there are any limitations, but after creating a new course and importing a PGN of my analysis, I was soon happily scoring points while rediscovering my openings! Well worth investigating if, like me, you're looking for a less dreary way to remember your analysis!

■ ■ ■

From the serious business of drilling opening preparation to the romantic creativity of a bygone age! This month has seen the release of two books about some free spirits of the pre-computer age: *The Livonian Knight – Selected Games of Alvis Vitolins* by Zigurds Lanka, Edvins Kengis, Janis Klovans and Janis Vitomskis (Elk and Ruby) and *U cannot be serious* by Gerard Welling and Mike Basman (Thinkers Publishing).

The Livonian Knight is an English-language version of a book first published in Latvia in 2008 (which

Sosonko's foreword that Tal often said (rubbing his hands together), 'And now let's play like Vitolins...' when sacrificing material in analysis!

The impressive or even unnerving thing about Vitolins' opening ideas is that it is hard to really categorise them or find a strategical thread running through them (as I believe you can in Basman's ideas). You feel he really could find something unexpectedly active in virtually any opening. For example:
1.d4 ♘f6 2.c4 e6 3.♘c3 ♗b4 4.♕c2 b5 5.cxb5 a6.

Vitolins played these Benko-type ideas in the Nimzo-Indian in various settings. The line 4.♕c2 0-0 5.a3 ♗xc3+ 6.♕xc3 b5 is respectable for

The Livonian Knight
Selected Games of
Alvis Vitolins
Lanka, Kengis,
Klovans & Vitomskis
Elk and Ruby, 2021
★★★☆☆

Or 1.d4 ♘f6 2.c4 e6 3.♘c3 ♗b4 4.e3 0-0 5.♘ge2 b5.

Vitolins took on the Latvian Alekhine experts of the time (such as Bagirov and Kengis) with the following shocking idea:
1.e4 ♘f6 2.e5 ♘d5 3.d4 d6 4.♘f3 ♗g4 5.c4 ♘b6 6.d5.

All-in-all, a lovely little book! I'm hesitating between 3 and 4 stars, but I'll stick with 3. Well worth getting: a short, joyful outburst of attacking play!

■ ■ ■

The inventive English IM Michael Basman turned 75 in March this year, an event that Thinkers Publishing have marked by bringing out *U cannot be serious* (co-authored

Tal often said (rubbing his hands together), 'And now let's play like Vitolins...' when sacrificing material in analysis!

I also have!) covering the games of the fantastic attacking talent Alvis Vitolins (1946-1997), who failed to fulfil his full playing potential but left a series of breath-taking attacking games and astounding opening ideas. This slim 124-page book analyses 25 of his best games, with biographical details and reminiscences of him by his Latvian colleagues interspersed among the notes. His forte was the Open Sicilian and in particular the sacrifice of something on b5 so it's not surprising to learn in Genna

Black, but I hadn't seen any of these ideas before:
1.d4 ♘f6 2.c4 e6 3.♘c3 ♗b4 4.♘f3 c5 5.g3 b5.

by Gerard Welling and Basman himself), bringing together many of Basman's crazy ideas and games in one volume. Basman was part of the super-strong group of English players that emerged in the 1970s and was famously characterised by Botvinnik as a creative and talented player. Basman didn't quite fulfil that promise but still became an IM and from the late 1970s he started on a path of opening experimentation that he never abandoned. Many of the English players of that

Obviously, these openings are dodgy and engine evaluations will inevitably be generally depressing

generation, such as Keene, Miles and Speelman, dabbled regularly in offbeat openings like Owen's Defence (1...b6), but Basman went the extra mile by standardising his repertoire on the St. George (1.e4 e6 2.d4 a6 followed by ...b5) or 1.a3 followed by 2.b4 as White, the Grob (1.g4), the Borg (1.e4 g5), eventually graduating to the Global openings a.k.a. 'Creepy Crawly' (1.a3 followed by 2.h3 or 1...a6 followed by 2...h6).

Perhaps surprisingly, I don't think Basman ever gained any followers in the UK: at least, I can't think of any strong players who regularly adopted his openings, despite all the effort that Basman put into popularising them with books (I still have my copy of his 1983 Pergamon book *Play the St. George* as a treasured possession) and audio tapes.

Basman remained a one-off, and that perhaps shows that part of the reason for his successes with this repertoire was that he was an

U cannot be serious
Gerard Welling &
Mike Basman
Thinkers Publishing,
2021
★★☆☆☆

extremely versatile player. You were never quite sure what Basman was aiming for when he played his openings: he was just as likely to settle for a pleasant ending as press for a crazy attack. For example, this game against strong junior and later grandmaster Aaron Summerscale made a strong impression on me – I'm fairly certain I saw it unfold live at the Lloyds Bank Masters in 1989.

Michael Basman
Aaron Summerscale
London Lloyds Bank 1989
1.g4 d5 2.h3 e5 3.♗g2 ♞c6 4.c4 dxc4 5.♗xc6+ bxc6 6.♞f3

6...h5 7.gxh5 e4 8.♞e5 ♛d5 9.♛a4 e3

10.f3 ♞e7 11.♞xc4 exd2+

12.♗xd2 ♗e6 13.♞ba3 ♞c8 14.e4 ♛d7 15.♞e5 ♛d6 16.♖c1 ♞b6 17.♛xc6+ ♛xc6 18.♞xc6

A totally bizarre opening, that Basman happily steered to a better ending that he won without any difficulty. It seemed like magic to me at the time (I was 15 and still very impressionable!).

U cannot be serious starts off with some reminiscences by Gerard Welling about Basman's participation in Biel 1979 and Liège 1981, and then we move into the theoretical sections examining the current state of opening theory in the St. George, the Grob and the Global openings before ending with a chapter showing some of Basman's most recent games.

I loved the opening chapters, in which Welling describes the effect that Basman's participation in Biel 1979 and Liège 1981 had on him and the other players. I could have read a whole book on this theme about the mystification of his opponents, the (fake?) outrage, the failed experiments, and the glorious victories! However, the book is considerably less successful when it moves on to the theoretical chapters. I wondered whether I'd misunderstood the purpose of these chapters but Welling describes them as detailing the 'current state of Basmanic theory' so I guess we do have to judge them according to modern standards.

Obviously, these openings are dodgy and engine evaluations will inevitably be generally depressing. This is something that I'm happy to ignore as a reader, losing myself in the creativity and trusting that the Basmanic confusion generated would be more than enough for many of my human opponents! The games are great from that point of view. However, many of the variations and evaluations bear little connection to the actual board situation, so much so that they jumped out at me while reading the book without a board. Some examples from one page:

1.e4 e6 2.d4 a6 3.♘f3 b5 4.♗d3 c5 5.c3 ♗b7 6.0-0 ♘f6 7.♖e1

This is one of White's best lines against the St. George. Black faces a development dilemma; castling would be advisable sometime soon, but ...♗e7 will lose a tempo after dxc5 ♗xc5. Ideally, Black would find a development scheme that would tempt White to capture on c5 before Black plays ...♗e7, but it's hard to suggest anything short of hypnotism! Apart from the main line 7...♕b6, Basman and Welling give some variations for 7...h6 and 7...♗e7 (anyway).

7...h6

On the same page, Basman and Welling give this line: 7...♗e7 8.♘bd2 ♘c6 9.e5 ♘d5 10.dxc5 ♗xc5 11.♘e4 ♗e7 12.a4 ♕b8 13.♘g3 (13.♗g5 is mentioned as an alternative, without comment, which is odd because Basman examines it in some detail in his *Play the St. George* as it was played against him by Andrew Lewis on the same day that Miles infamously defeated Karpov with 1...a6 and 2...b5! White was clearly better and Basman started to look for improvements at a much earlier stage) 13...g5

ANALYSIS DIAGRAM

and now both 14.♘xg5 and 14.h3 are examined, ending in unclear positions or winning positions for Black. However, what about 14.♗xg5 ? I appreciate the inventiveness behind 13...g5, and it is very typical of Basman to undermine White's centre with unexpected wing-pawn thrusts, but this is simply catastrophic: 14...♗xg5 15.♘xg5 ♕xe5 16.♗e4 and the black king is caught in the centre, with no hopes of counterplay.

The book is well worth getting but beware of following the analysis!

8.♘bd2 ♗e7 9.e5 ♘d5 10.dxc5 ♗xc5 11.♘e4 ♗e7 12.a4 bxa4 13.♖xa4 ♘c6 14.♗b1 ♘b6 15.♖a1 ♘c4

This is given as unclear with the comment 'The reader is invited to do further investigation here'. However, 16.♕b3 simply wins a piece.

16.♕b3 ♘6a5

16...♘4a5 17.♕a2, with b4 to follow.

17.♕a2 With b3 to follow.

Magnus Carlsen's most instructive games
Martyn Kravtsiv
Gambit, 2021
★★★★☆

I'm somewhat torn by this book. I'm an enthusiast of these lines, Basman is very much a part of my English chess heritage and I think it's lovely that a book has been produced about his unique approach to chess. However, I was extremely disappointed by the level of analysis, which turned my reading experience a little sour. I'm going to go for 2 stars, with the comment that it's well worth getting but beware of following the analysis!

■ ■ ■

Back to the sublime now, as Ukrainian Grandmaster Martyn Kravtsiv analyses *Magnus Carlsen's Most Instructive Games* (Gambit). Each of the 42 games (played at classical, rapid and blitz time-controls) has been selected to illustrate a specific theme, divided up into Opening Themes, Middlegame Topics, Endgame Play and Human Factors. A nice touch is the 'Magnus moment', highlighted in every game, where Kravtsiv spotlights a particularly fine idea by the World Champion.

This works extremely well as a learning technique: a few of those positions have already stuck in my mind even after a single read! I also think the thematic approach to Magnus' games works very well and gives the book a structure and cohesion that a simple games collection might not achieve. It's a professional and instructive attempt to draw lessons from the games of the strongest human player on the planet! 4 stars!

■ ■ ■

Finally, another offering from the Soviet archives, brought to you once again by Elk and Ruby: *Selected Games – Peter Romanovsky*. The first part is an exhaustive biography of Romanovsky's (1892-1964) chess life, tracing tournament results from 1909 to 1951. Twice Soviet champion and an ever-present figure in Soviet chess life for more than 40 years, he was probably at his strongest between 1925 and 1935. In those years he shared 7th-8th in the 1st Moscow International Tournament in 1925 and 8th-10th in the 2nd Moscow International Tournament of 1935, which gives an idea of his approximate strength compared to the best Western players. He also wrote 16 books, contributed regularly to many different magazines, taught many generations of children, and acted as an arbiter towards the end of his life. And of course, inevitably for someone

Romanovsky is not my favourite player of that era, but I do like his annotations

who lived in this tumultuous period in world history, he suffered heartbreaking personal tragedy, losing his entire family (wife and four daughters) in January 1942 within the space of 20 days. Inevitably for someone of his prickly temperament, he also fell out several times with the chess authorities, which in those times was a somewhat risky thing to do.

Romanovsky is not my favourite player of that era, but I do like his annotations. A few years ago, Quality Chess published a new edition of his middlegame guide *Soviet Middlegame Technique* which I liked very much. It's not that you agree with everything, and many of the judgements seem naive or outdated to modern eyes, but Romanovsky's overwhelming desire to draw lessons

Selected Games – Peter Romanovsky
Tkachenko & Bogdanovich
Elk and Ruby, 2021
★★★★☆

from his study – questioning every assumption, including those he made himself at an earlier stage! – and to teach others, shines through every sentence, which make his writings inspiring to read.

I'll finish with one of his most famous combinations. The circumstances were quite funny. Feeling unwell, Romanovsky had decided not to turn up for the game (against his eternal nemesis Ilya Rabinovich), but his friends persuaded him to play. Turning up an hour and a quarter late for the game, Romanovsky had 45 minutes to play his first 30 moves. He was in a somewhat manic state of mind and played extremely aggressively. In this position, Rabinovich had just played 17.e5:

Ilya Rabinovich
Peter Romanovsky
Moscow 1925

position after 17.e5

Rabinovich admitted after the game that he was expecting Romanovsky to resign and that the idea that he would be the one mated a few moves later had never crossed his mind!

17...♗a3 Total bluff and confusion... and it works!

18.exf6 After this unnecessary capture, White is suddenly on the back foot!

18.♘e1, challenging the bishop on d3, or 18.♕a4, challenging the bishop on a3 while leaving the capture of the knight on f6 for later, were very strong for White.

18...♕c5 19.♗d2 ♗g6

A devilish move, preparing ...♕f5 with mate on c2!

20.♕a4 b5

20...♖xd2 was the better move, according to my engine: 21.♖xd2 (21.♔xd2 ♕xf2+ 22.♘e2 ♗c5 23.♘fd4 e5 24.♖hf1 ♕h4 and Black will pick up the knight on d4 with a raging attack) 21...♕xc3+ 22.♔d1 ♗xb2 23.♔e2 ♗c1 24.♖d7 ♕b2+ 25.♔f1 gxf6 with the two bishops and two pawns for the exchange. However, Romanovsky's choice is much trickier, giving White multiple opportunities to go wrong!

21.♕xa3 21.♕xb5 ♖ab8 22.♕xc5 ♗xb2 mate. Aaah!;

21.♕b3 b4 22.bxa3 bxc3 23.♗e3 ♕c7 24.♘d4 is one of the engine lines that ends in 0.00! However, in raging time-trouble, I think a human player would find it hard to be sure about that! The only way you could choose it under those circumstances is by elimination: everything else loses immediately, this doesn't so let's play it! However, Rabinovich had missed an important detail!

21...♕f5

22.♕b3 ♖ac8

0-1. Despite two extra pieces, White has no way to prevent ...♕b1 mate. Another lovely slice of chess history! 4 stars! ∎

Jan Timman

A Fearless Youngster

Although he failed to qualify for the knockouts, Praggnanandhaa easily held his own against the world top in the preliminaries of the New In Chess Classic. **JAN TIMMAN** describes the young Indian player's style as 'strategically sound, tactically alert, and sharp'. And he is fearless. Even against the World Champion he kept looking for chances to play for a win.

Twice before the young Indian star Rameshbabu Praggnanandhaa was the focus of attention in this magazine. In a profile in New In Chess 2017/6, V. Saravanan wondered if 'Pragga' (who made his debut as a commentator analysing two of his games for the article) would manage to beat Sergey Karjakin's record of 12 years and 7 months to become the youngest grandmaster in history (he didn't – in the end he needed 3 months and 13 days more). Then in New In Chess 2019/6, I wrote about the sensational victory of the 13-year-old prodigy in the Xtracon Open in Helsingor, Denmark – a milestone in his career.

Early last year, at 17 years of age, Pragga crossed the 2600 line. And this is where things are still at now. At the start of the lockdown, he was on 2608, but he has not played a single classical game since.

In my Editorial in Yearbook 135, I already voiced my worries that the lockdown might get in the way of the continued development of young players like Alireza Firouzja and Jorden van Foreest. This worry proved unfounded, as witness the outcome of, for example, Wijk aan Zee. And it seems that Praggnanandhaa has also continued to develop excellently. He was successful in online tournaments, and I was curious to see how he would do in the New In Chess Classic. I was certainly not disappointed. Although the young Indian failed to qualify for the knockouts, he completely held his own against the world top in the preliminaries.

He also showed a good attitude, as in his second-round game against the Polish number one.

At the start of the lockdown, Praggnanandhaa was on 2608, but he has not played a single classical game since

Jan-Krzysztof Duda
Rameshbabu Praggnanandhaa
New In Chess Classic 2021 (prelim 1)

position after 29.♘d6

White has a strong knight, but Black can undermine its position in two ways.

29...f6 Objectively, 29...c5 was the correct move. After 30.dxc5 ♘xe5 31.♕e4 f5 Black will be able to hold.
30.♖b1 c5 31.♖b7
The wrong piece! With 31.♘b7! White could have netted the c-pawn. White has bigger fish to fry, but as a result has overlooked a venomous finesse.

31...♘xe5! Elegant and sharp.
32.♕xd5

Black did not need to fear the consequences of 32.dxe5 ♖xd1+ 33.♔g2 ♖xd6. The text-move will liquidate to an equal endgame.

32...exd5 33.♖xd7 ♘xd7 34.♘b7 ♖c8 35.dxc5 ♖c7 36.c6 ♘b6 37.♘a5 ♔f7 38.♔g2 ♔e6 39.♘b7 ♔e5 An extremely risky winning attempt, which will work out in the end. With other moves, e.g. 39...♘c4, Black could easily have preserved the balance.

40.♖e1+

And now Black gets his way. His king will penetrate to support the passed d-pawn.

Far stronger was 40.f4+!, when the black king has no good squares, e.g. 40...♔e4 41.♘c5+ ♔f5 42.♘b3!, and the knight will support the c-pawn from d4. White has a winning advantage.

40...♔d4 41.♘d8 ♔d3!

The king is a strong piece, especially in the endgame.

42.♖e3+

This panicky check leads to defeat. White could have saved himself with 42.♖c1 ♘c4 43.♖d1+ ♘d2 44.♖c1.

42...♔d2 43.♖e6

On his way up. Rameshbabu Praggnanandhaa completely held his own against the world top in the preliminaries of the New In Chess Classic.

43...♘c4! Keeping the white rook from d6. Now White is powerless against the advancing d-pawn.

44.f4 ♔c3 45.♘b7 d4 46.♘d6 ♘xd6 47.♖xd6 d3 48.♔f2 d2 49.♔f3 ♔c2 50.♔e4 ♖e7+ White resigned.

Against Sergey Karjakin, Praggnanandhaa won a game that was both strategically and tactically solid.

Rameshbabu Praggnanandhaa
Sergey Karjakin
New In Chess Classic 2021 (prelim 5)
Queen's Indian, Nimzowitsch Variation

1.d4 ♘f6 2.c4 e6 3.♘f3 b6 4.g3 ♗a6 5.b3 ♗b4+ 6.♗d2 ♗e7 7.♘c3 d5 8.cxd5 exd5 9.♗g2 0-0 10.0-0 ♗b7 11.♘e5 ♘bd7 12.♗f4 ♖e8 13.♖c1 ♘f8

14.♘b5

This sortie is pointless. The standard move is 14.♗g5, as in Petrosian-Kortchnoi, Il Ciocco 1977, and Portisch-Sosonko, Tilburg 1984. The plan is 14...♘e6 15.♗xf6 ♗xf6 16.e3, and White had a slight strategic plus in both games. 16...c5 is probably Black's best reaction, leaving White with nothing tangible.

14...♘e6 15.♘c6 ♕d7 16.♘xe7+ ♖xe7 17.♘c3 ♘xf4 18.gxf4 a5

The opening has gone well for Black, but 18...♖ae8 would have been stronger. After 19.e3 ♗a6 20.♖e1 c6 Black has a comfortable position.

19.e3 ♗a6 20.♖e1 ♖d8 21.♖c2 g6 22.♕d2 h5 23.♖ec1

23...h4 Karjakin's rook pawn moves are not great. This one will eventually cost him control of the g4-square, albeit not immediately. 23...♔g7 would have been more accurate.

24.h3 ♕f5 25.♘a4 ♖dd7

26.♕d1! Little moves like this one betray Praggnanandhaa's major talent. From d1, the queen will be able to sortie to the kingside.

26...♔g7

Black had an improbable way to keep the balance: 26...♘d3 27.♖d2 ♗e4 28.f3, and now 28...♗b1!. If White takes the bishop, he will lose two pawns and be left in a dubious strategic position. After 29.♖c3 b5 30.♘c5 ♖d8 Black will also have sufficient counterplay.

27.♘b2 ♔h6 28.♖c6 ♗b5 29.♖6c2 ♗a6 30.♔h2 ♔g7 31.♗f1 ♗xf1 32.♕xf1 ♘e4 33.♖c6 ♔f8 34.♘d3 f6 35.♖1c2 ♔e8 36.♕g2 ♘d6

37.♘e5!?

An interesting and practically justified sacrifice: both players had about three minutes left. The text does not upset the balance, but it does make it very hard for Black to defend with so little time on the clock.

The modest 37.♘e1 would have preserved White's strategic plus.

37...fxe5 38.dxe5 ♘e4

38...d4 39.exd6 dxe3 was another possibility. The position is equal, but this was hard to see with so little time left.

39.♖xg6 ♔d8

40.♖g8+ The alternative was 40.♕g4, creating as strong a pawn front as possible. After 40...♕xg4 41.hxg4 ♘c5 42.♖g8+ ♖e8 43.♖xe8+ ♔xe8 44.f5 ♘e4 Black will just about hold.

40...♖e8 41.♖xe8+ ♔xe8 42.♕g8+ ♕f8 43.♕e6+ ♔d8 44.♕c6 ♘c5 45.♖c1 d4

Good enough. But 45...♕f5 46.♖g1 ♘e6 would also have given Black a solid defensive line.

46.♖g1

46...d3?

Karjakin collapses under the pressure. His only move was 46...♔e7, when the position is equal but the battle remains sharp. A possible continuation would be 47.♕f3 d3 48.f5 d2 49.f6+ ♔e8 50.♕h5+ ♔d8 51.♕f3, and the black king has to return to e8.

47.♖g8! The decisive blow.

47...♕xg8 48.♕a8+ ♔e7 49.♕xg8 ♖d8 50.♕g7+ ♔e6 51.f5+ ♔d5 52.e6

Black resigned.

Praggnanandhaa's style has not crystallized out yet, but it's already possible to see some characteristics: strategically sound, tactically alert, and sharp. These characteristics also came to the fore in his game against Teimour Radjabov.

Rameshbabu Praggnanandhaa
Teimour Radjabov
New In Chess Classic 2021 (prelim 9)
Queen's Gambit Declined

1.d4 ♘f6 2.c4 e6 3.♘f3 d5 4.♘c3 ♗e7 5.♗f4 0-0 6.e3 ♘bd7 7.c5 ♘h5 8.♗d3 ♘xf4 9.exf4 b6 10.b4 a5 11.a3 c6 12.0-0

12...♕c7

In Ding Liren-Grischuk, Yekaterinburg 2021, there followed 12...♗a6 13.♗xa6 ♖xa6, and now White played 14.♘e2, a move that the computer doesn't think much of. But Ding Liren still managed to win the game! Radjabov had played the text earlier.

13.g3 ♗a6 14.♗xa6 ♖xa6 15.♕e2

In a rapid game in the Skilling Open last year, Nakamura played 15.♖e1 against Radjabov, getting nowhere. Praggnanandhaa had undoubtedly prepared the text.

15...♖a7 16.f5

This is not a new idea, of course, but White has played it for a special purpose.

16...axb4

16...e5 at once would probably have been more accurate. After 17.cxb6 ♕xb6 18.dxe5 axb4 19.axb4 ♗xb4 White can retain some advantage with 20.♘a2 ♗c5 21.♖ab1.

17.axb4 ♖xa1 18.♖xa1 e5 19.♘xe5 ♘xe5 20.dxe5 bxc5

21.b5!

Sharp thinking. White continues to restrict the black bishop's range.

21...d4 22.b6!

And this is the real point of White's 17th move. The black queen is distracted to allow White to take his knight to e4.

22...♕xb6 23.♘e4 f6

24.e6

Strategically played, but the march of the e-pawn will not end up yielding an advantage. The alternative was 24.♕c4+, in order to penetrate with the queen, which was objectively stronger. After 24...♔h8 25.♕e6 ♕c7 26.exf6 gxf6 27.♖a6 Black won't have it easy, e.g. 27...d3 28.♖xc6 ♕d8 29.♘d2, and White is better.

24...♕b5 25.♕a2 ♕d3

Simpler was 25...c4, since after 26.♕a7 ♕xf5 27.♕xe7 ♕xe4 White would have been forced to settle for a draw immediately.

26.♕a7 ♕xe4 27.♕xe7 ♕xf5 28.h4 ♕g4 29.♖a7 h5 30.♖d7

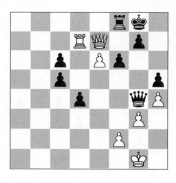

30...♖a8?

A slip of concentration. Radjabov probably briefly forgot that he has too few checks in this specific position. A good move was 30...♕g6, since 31.♖d8 ♖xd8 32.♕xd8+ ♔h7 33.e7 would be met by 33...♕b1+

34.♔g2 ♕e4+, with perpetual check. 30...♕d1+ 31.♔g2 ♕g4 would also have sufficed, because it would have given Black another check on e4.

31.♖d8+ ♖xd8 32.♕xd8+ ♔h7 33.e7

Black resigned. He will run out of checks after 33...♕d1+ 34.♔g2.

Against Hikaru Nakamura, Praggnanandhaa tried for a long time to convert his endgame advantage.

Hikaru Nakamura
Rameshbabu Praggnanandhaa
New In Chess Classic 2021 (prelim 14)

position after 24...♘d6

White will lose his b-pawn. What is the best way to give it up?

25.e3

Obvious but not best. Stronger was 25.b6!, which gives Black a passed b-pawn that is far less dangerous than the rook pawn. After 25...axb6 26.e3 e5 27.♘b3 the position is equal. An instructive moment!

25...♘xb5 26.♔g2

26...♘c3

Obvious; but 26...♘d6, restricting the activity of the white pieces,

would have been stronger. A possible continuation is 27.♘b3 ♖b1 28.♘c5 a5 29.♗d3 ♖c1 30.♘a4 ♘c4 31.♘d4 ♖a1 32.♘c3 ♖b2 33.♗c2 g5, and Black retains winning chances.

27.♘c4

An important move: the black a-pawn is stopped for the moment.

27...♖a1 28.♘d4 ♖a2 29.♗d3 a5 30.♘c2

30...a4

30...♘a4 would have preserved practical chances for Black, although White will be able to hold, e.g. 31.♘4a3 ♘c5 32.♗c4 ♖b2 33.♔f1. After the text Black will eventually lose his passed pawn.

31.♔f1 e5 32.f3 ♘d5 33.♔e1 a3 34.♔d1 ♖xc2 35.♗xh7+

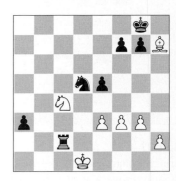

This is how White can save himself in a knight ending. Praggnanandhaa continues to press for a very long time.

35...♔xh7 36.♔xc2 e4 37.fxe4 a2 38.♔b2 ♘c3 39.♘d2 ♔g6 40.♘f3 ♔f6 41.♔a1 g5 42.g4 ♘xe4 43.♔xa2 ♘f2 44.♔b3 ♘xg4 45.h4 gxh4 46.♘xh4 ♘xe3 47.♔c3 ♘g5 48.♘f3+ ♔f4 49.♘d4 ♔e4 50.♘b5 ♘f5 51.♔d2 ♔f3 52.♔d3 ♘g3 53.♘d6 f6 54.♘e8 f5 55.♘g7 ♔f4 56.♘xf5 ♔xf5

Draw.

Magnus Carlsen had this to say about Praggnanandhaa's performance in the New In Chess Classic: 'I think we can enjoy the fact that he's playing so well at his age. I would also say, fearlessly. He certainly didn't show me too much respect when we were playing.' And it's true that the young Indian consistently played for a win against him, and that the World Champion had to watch his step at some point:

Rameshbabu Praggnanandhaa
Magnus Carlsen
New In Chess Classic 2021 (prelim 13)

position after 24...♘e4

White is a pawn up, but it is clear that he won't be able to keep it.
25.♖b7 His best chance. **25...♖ac8** With 25...♖cc8 Black could have avoided all problems. The four-rook endgame arising after this won't offer White any winning chances.
26.♖xc7 ♖xc7

27.♖b4 Now Black's problem is that he won't be able to capture on c5.
27...♘xc3 28.♖c4 ♘d5 29.♖a4 ♖c6 30.♖a5 White still has some pressure. His passed c-pawn is not entirely harmless.

30...f6 31.f4 h6 32.♔f2 g5 33.g3 gxf4 34.gxf4 ♔f7

35.♔f3 The alternative was 35.a3, intending to take the knight to b4, when Black will just manage to hold: 35...♔g6 36.♘b4 ♘xb4 37.axb4 ♔f5 38.♔e3 e5 39.fxe5 ♔xe5. The white king cannot penetrate.
35...♔g6 36.♔e4 ♘c3+ 37.♔e3 ♘d5+ 38.♔e4 ♘c3+ 39.♔d4 ♘d5

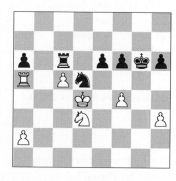

40.♖a4! With a clear plan: White is going to force a knight swap.
40...♔f5 41.♘b4 ♘xb4 42.♖xb4 ♖c8! The only move. The rook must be activated.
43.♖b6 e5+ Again the only option.
44.fxe5 fxe5+ 45.♔d5 e4 46.c6 e3 47.♖b1 e2

48.♖e1
A good practical move that forces Black to be accurate.
The alternative 48.♔d6 offered better winning chances, however, as witness 48...♖d8+ 49.♔c5 ♖d2 50.c7 ♔e5 51.♔c6 ♖d6+ 52.♔b7 ♖d1 53.♖b3, and Black must allow both sides to queen in favourable circumstances for White. After 53...e1♕ 54.c8♕

Magnus Carlsen on Praggnanandhaa: 'He certainly didn't show me too much respect when we were playing'

♕e4+ 55.♔a7 ♕d4+ 56.♖b6 Black will not have it easy.
48...♖d8+!
Certainly not 48...♖e8, in view of 49.c7, followed by capturing on e2.
49.♔c5 ♖d2

That was the idea of the previous move. Black can now continue to check the white king, keeping the c-pawn from getting dangerous. Praggnanandhaa kept trying different things for thirty more moves, persistently looking for ways to beat the World Champion, but to no avail. Eventually he had to cease his efforts and settle for a draw (½-½, 80). ■

Vincent Keymer

CURRENT ELO: 2591

DATE OF BIRTH: November 15, 2004

PLACE OF BIRTH: Mainz, Germany

PLACE OF RESIDENCE: Saulheim, Germany

What is your favourite city?
Vienna.

What was the last great meal you had?
Indian food during my holidays last summer.

What drink brings a smile to your face?
Jasmine tea.

Which book would you give to a friend?
Ian McEwan, *Machines like me*.

What book is currently on your bedside table?
Shakespeare, *Macbeth* (for school).

What is your all-time favourite movie?
The First Grader.

And your favourite TV series?
Dr. House.

Do you have a favourite actor?
Jack Nicholson.

And a favourite actress?
Barbara Streisand.

What music do you listen to?
Music pieces that my parents and my sister practise. ☺

Is there a painting that moves you?
Max Ernst, *Der Vogel im Wald*.

What is your earliest chess memory?
Dr. Helmut Pfleger's videos on famous chess games.

Who is your favourite chess player of all time?
I don't have one. My first strong impressions came from Anand and Kasparov.

Is there a chess book that had a profound influence on you?
Garry Kasparov, *My Great Predecessors*.

What was your best result ever?
Winning the 2018 Grenke Open.

And the best game you played?
Keymer-Gelfand, Isle of Man 2018.

What was the most exciting chess game you ever saw?
A recent game that comes to mind is Caruana-Duda, Wijk aan Zee 2021.

What is your favourite square?
h7, because of the many beautiful sacrifices that happen there.

Do chess players have typical shortcomings?
Impatience.

What are chess players particularly good at (except for chess)?
Making plans.

Do you have any superstitions concerning chess?
Keeping the same pen after a good result/changing it after a bad one.

Facebook, Instagram, Snapchat, or?
None.

Who do you follow on Twitter?
No one.

What is your life motto?
Still searching for a good one.

Who or what would you like to be if you weren't yourself?
A kangaroo.

When was the last time you cried?
After eating too many lemons.

Which three people would you like to invite for dinner?
Asterix, Obelix and one Roman. ☺

What is the best piece of advice you were ever given?
It is better to fail than to have never even tried.

Is there something you'd love to learn?
More foreign languages.

What would people be surprised to know about you?
Although I spend a lot of time on chess, I am still going to school.

Where is your favourite place in the world?
The vineyards around my village.

What is your greatest fear?
To oversleep before an important game.

And your greatest regret?
Not to have more time for playing piano.

If you could change one thing in the chess world, what would it be?
Eliminate cheating.

What does it mean to be a chess player?
A lot of hard work and determination.

What is the best thing that was ever said about chess?
Emanuel Lasker: Without mistakes there is no brilliance.